Praise for
Ready to Rise

"Jo Saxton's voice on leadership is bold, urgent, and full of grace. She calls us to challenge our preconceived notions about leadership and influence, to question the lies we've believed, and to rediscover the calling of God. This book is an invitation to rise into the fullness of whom God made each of us to be and to remember that we do our best rising together."

> —AMENA BROWN, poet, author, and host of *HER with Amena Brown* podcast

"Our ability as women to own, shape, and steward our experiences and stories will directly influence how whole and healed our communities can be. In a world brimming with hopelessness, brokenness, and sin, this is the exact book we need to fully step into our leadership to restore not only our broken communities but our broken selves in the process."

> —JENNY YANG, vice president of advocacy and policy at World Relief

"Jo is a catalytic leader who wants to see you lead in all areas of your life—shaping culture and bringing God's love, truth, healing, and transformation wherever you go."

> —ANDI ANDREW, author of *She Is Free* and *Fake or Follower*

"*Ready to Rise* is the winning combination of an honest friend, challenging preacher, and inspiring leadership coach. If you're ready to be blown way with what God can do with your life, I dare you to take action on the lessons learned from *Ready to Rise*."

—MEGAN TAMTE, founder and co-CEO of Evereve

"This is a book every woman needs to read, providing hard-won lessons on how to rise above what holds us back and offering a game plan to thrive in our callings. The wisdom, tools, and powerful encouragement will change your life!"

—ALLI WORTHINGTON, bestselling author, speaker, and
cofounder of Called Creatives

"Through biblical stories and perspectives, Jo empowers you to get up and show up for what you were created to do."

—ALLIE CASAZZA, host of *The Purpose Show*

"Jo reminds us that when we boldly step into our lives, we create a legacy for those coming after us. Jo's words are an encouragement for us to walk into the unknown—with confidence that Christ has commissioned us all to *rise up*."

—JESSICA HONEGGER, founder and co-CEO of Noonday
Collection and author of *Imperfect Courage*

"Jo Saxton, through a refreshingly real and vulnerable telling of her own journey, unabashedly captures the various intersections women leaders are conditioned to navigate. Saxton offers her readers an empowering alternative to the often-toxic narratives that have shaped many women in these spaces."

—REV. GAIL SONG BANTUM, lead pastor of Quest Church

"*Ready to Rise* is compelling, honest, and powerful. Jo's retelling of Deborah from Judges is one of the best I've ever read. This is a book for men and women, people of all ages and ethnicities."

—Jo Anne Lyon, ambassador, general superintendent emerita, the Wesleyan Church

"At a time when many are afraid to use their voices, gifts, and talents, we must understand how our lives are intricately connected. 'Sometimes our voices are needed for courageous conversations. Sometimes our voices give other people the courage to find theirs.' Who might be waiting for you to use your voice and leverage your influence? *Ready to Rise* inspires a generation to take our place in the midst of doubt and chaos and lead with full confidence."

—Latasha Morrison, author and founder of Be the Bridge

"This book isn't about platform, opportunity, or how to get ahead; it's about the heart of a woman and the words we've needed to hear for centuries. From heartwarming personal stories, authentic dialogues, and accurate biblical foundation, *Ready to Rise* will help women all across the globe find their voices—and keep them."

—Toni J. Collier, communicator, host, and consultant

"Jo Saxton's voice is one that continues to rise above the self-help fray. While the messages of today have us careening between Too Much and Not Enough, Jo's words are a balm and the gentle but firm encouragement we need to rise. I'm ready."

—Liz Forkin Bohannon, founder of Sseko Designs and author of *Beginner's Pluck*

"Jo embodies this book, and I'm grateful to call her a friend and learn how to lead better because of her influence in my life!"

—TYLER REAGIN, author of *The Life-Giving Leader*

"When Jo Saxton speaks, I listen. From stages and written pages, Jo tells the truth with wisdom, authenticity, grit, hope, and life-giving grace. Read. This. Book."

—DANIELLE STRICKLAND, founder of Women Speakers Collective, writer, and activist

"*Ready to Rise* is a dynamic book filled with wisdom for every woman who wants to align with God's plan and spread infectious light in the world."

—SYBIL CLARK-AMUTI, founder of *The Great Girlfriends* podcast

"We all win as leaders when our teams are empowered to bring their gifts and abilities to the table, and we all lose when they are held back. Jo unpacks this critical leadership concept and brings it home in the delightful style only Jo Saxton can deliver. Go buy this book for yourself and then for everyone on your team. You won't regret it."

—MELISSA K. RUSSELL, president, North America, International Justice Mission

Jo Saxton

READY TO RISE

Own *Your* Voice

Gather *Your* Community

Step into *Your* Influence

WATERBROOK

All Scripture quotations, unless otherwise indicated, are taken from the Holy Bible, New International Version®, NIV®. Copyright © 1973, 1978, 1984, 2011 by Biblica Inc.® Used by permission. All rights reserved worldwide. Scripture quotations marked (NLT) are taken from the Holy Bible, New Living Translation, copyright © 1996, 2004, 2007, 2013, 2015 by Tyndale House Foundation. Used by permission of Tyndale House Publishers Inc., Carol Stream, Illinois 60188. All rights reserved. Scripture quotations marked (TPT) are taken from The Passion Translation®. Copyright © 2017, 2018 by Passion & Fire Ministries, Inc. Used by permission. All rights reserved. ThePassionTranslation.com.

Details and names in some anecdotes and stories have been changed to protect the identities of the persons involved.

Trade Paperback ISBN 978-0-7352-8984-0
eBook ISBN 978-0-7352-8985-7

Published in the United States by WaterBrook, an imprint of Random House, a division of Penguin Random House LLC.

WaterBrook® and its deer colophon are registered trademarks of Penguin Random House LLC.

Library of Congress Cataloging-in-Publication Data
Names: Saxton, Jo, 1974- author.
Title: Ready to rise : own your voice, gather your community, step into your influence / Jo Saxton.
Description: First edition. | Colorado Springs : WaterBrook, an imprint of Random House, a division of Penguin Random House LLC, 2020. | Includes bibliographical references.
Identifiers: LCCN 2019044544 | ISBN 9780735289840 (trade paperback) | ISBN 9780735289857 (ebook)
Subjects: LCSH: Christian women—Religious life. | Self-actualization (Psychology) in women. | Self-actualization (Psychology)—Religious aspects—Christianity. | Influence (Psychology)—Religious aspects—Christianity.
Classification: LCC BV4527 .S264 2020 | DDC 248.8/43—dc23
LC record available at https://lccn.loc.gov/2019044544

Printed in the United States of America
2020—First Edition

10 9 8 7 6 5 4 3 2 1

Special Sales
Most WaterBrook books are available at special quantity discounts when purchased in bulk by corporations, organizations, and special-interest groups. Custom imprinting or excerpting can also be done to fit special needs. For information, please email specialmarketscms@penguinrandomhouse.com.

In loving memory of Lisa Michelle Ganske,
who had the most infectious laugh and was
a woman of grit, grace, and kindness.
We miss you.

Contents

Introduction 1
**(A Seventh-Grade Girl Finds Her Voice and Speaks
   Truth to Power)**

1 Women Who've Made a Difference 5
(And Why I Wasn't Sure I Was One)

2 The Cost of Disempowerment 19
(And How I've Looked for Myself in All the Right Places)

3 Talitha Koum! 33
(And What Jesus Really Says About Women)

4 The Surprising Answer to "What Would Jesus Do?" 45
(And Why Pedicures Are Not Required)

5 Say Yes to Who You Are 57
(And Why We Don't Leave Good Gifts Unwrapped)

6 A Voice Without Apology 79
(And What "Too Much" Really Means)

7 Voice Lessons 95
(And When to Listen to Your Coaches)

8 How to Grow Your Grit 109
(It May Not Be Exactly How You Think)

9 Body Talk 125
(And How to Listen to What Your Body Is Saying)

10 The Search for Community 141
    (And All the Things That Stop Women from Having It)

11 How to Build Your Village 159
    (One Brick at a Time)

12 The Strategic Relationships Every Village Needs 171
    (You Might Feel Awkward About Them at First)

13 Ready to Shape a New Skyline? 185
    (On Your Mark . . .)

I Am Ready to Rise 199
Acknowledgments 201
Notes 203

Introduction

(A Seventh-Grade Girl Finds Her Voice and Speaks Truth to Power)

It's a broken world. I want to help fix it. I want to lead
the people who want to help fix it.

The school auditorium rippled with excitement. It was award night
for the seventh graders. On the stage, more than a hundred honors
students waited, familiar faces unfamiliarly dressed. In turns, they
mocked and admired one another's outfits, chatting animatedly in an
attempt to subdue their nerves and self-consciousness.

Across from the stage, the room was filled with their loved ones
until it was standing room only. Proud parents, even prouder grand-
parents, and loved ones posed and positioned cameras and smartphones, while others greeted one another, celebrating their children's achievements or confirming car-pool arrangements and sports

schedules. Younger siblings were being distracted by snacks or toys or the occasional tablet. The older ones entertained themselves with their own electronic devices, or they caught up with peers who'd also been brought along.

Meanwhile, the teaching staff milled around the auditorium, patiently trying to conduct sound checks on microphones and speakers that seemed to delight in jolting the audience with sudden and intrusively loud feedback. But then the principal took hold of a mic and cleared his throat to indicate the event was about to begin, and a hush fell over the room.

There were murmurs of surprise when the young woman's name was announced, because she hadn't told any of her friends that she was one of the two students selected to give a speech. Clutching her note cards, she made her way up to the podium and adjusted the microphone, perhaps because she felt it was the right thing to do.

She looked up and saw the number of people in the room and the anticipation on their faces. Spotting her parents, she exchanged a flickering glance with them and then determinedly looked down at her notes. She began speaking.

First, she thanked the families, parents, and teachers for both their presence and their contribution to her class's achievements. "This night belongs to you all," she said.

Then she spoke about her school journey—how she'd been shaped by experiences both positive and painful. She described the influence of teachers and friends who'd believed in her and encouraged her, thanking them for her growth. When she began speaking about harder times, she shared how difficult it had been to fill in a school survey that asked her to identify her ethnicity but didn't permit her to check more than one box. There just wasn't an option that reflected her biracial identity.

"I wondered why there wasn't a box for me," she said.

In fact, she'd called her mom in tears that day. "It's like I don't exist," she'd said, weeping.

Somehow, it was in this touch of vulnerability that her confidence seemed to grow. It was obvious the crowd was really warming to her, and she looked directly at the people in front of her. She indicated that she'd overcome her challenges by drawing strength from how her family had previously dealt with racially motivated incidents. She said that as she dreamed of the future, she didn't expect an easy or straightforward journey to achievement, but she wouldn't be deterred either.

"It's a broken world. I want to help fix it. I want to lead the people who want to help fix it."

After commending her peers and thanking parents and teachers again, she ended her speech to rapturous applause. There were many tear-stained but smiling faces in the audience.

She skipped back to her seat and to the company of her friends, took a deep breath, and smiled at me.

I didn't cry, but I *was* deeply moved. When she had used her seventh-grade mind and heart to speak truth to power, it wasn't just her confidence that had struck me, nor was it the tender vulnerability as she shared her story. Instead, it was the calm assumption with which she declared that she, that *we*, could play a role in changing a broken world. She simply believed that she, with everyone around her, had a contribution to make.

I leaned back into my chair, returned my daughter's smile, and thought, *That's my girl.*

Women Who've Made a Difference

(And Why I Wasn't Sure I Was One)

The path to our destination is not always a straight one.
We go down the wrong road, we get lost, we turn back.
Maybe it doesn't matter which road we embark on.
Maybe what matters is that we embark.

—BARBARA HALL

I reflected on my daughter's speech—her moment—for months. The lens through which she saw the world and the resolve to do something about it reminded me of a time years before: Her younger sister (aged five at the time) called a family meeting to announce what she wanted to be when she grew up. She told us she would be running for president and her agenda would involve taking care of the environment and protecting marine life. (She has since moved on to other career choices.)

Naturally, I love the budding ideas and dreams and passions my kids—two daughters—have, particularly as they develop and mature and learn more about the world around them. But while their enthusiasm—and their innocence—moves me, I am inspired by the liberated audacity of their assumption that they have something to offer, that they have a contribution to make in those places in the world that they believe are broken.

This is the message they constantly see around them—the mantras that say they can be who they want to be, that they can change the world, and that they can live meaningful and purposeful lives by helping and serving people. And, yes, there's certainly a dose of idealism, but this message of empowerment is also conveyed in the books they read about women who've made a difference. They're inspired by the way they see leaders—who remind them a little, or a lot, of themselves—grace the global stage. I'll always remember the day when my eldest was a toddler and saw President Barack Obama on TV. She jumped up and down, shouting, "Mommy! His skin! He's just like me!"

Seeing people who look like them and hearing people share stories similar to theirs has catalyzed my children's understanding of their own potential and purpose. And this is true for other children, not just mine. There's a generation growing up that seems to already know that to live a life that makes a meaningful impact is not only necessary but part of our design. And although it is marvelous to watch these young people grow with such purpose behind them, they're not the first to know this—not the first generation, or, to bring it much closer to home, not the first in our family.

The journey each generation embarks upon as they discover their influence and potential has been different from the previous, inevitably shaped by the times they were in. I've seen it over and over again, even in my own family. The generations of women who came before my daughters often discovered their purpose in ways they couldn't prepare for. Sometimes, their skills, callings, and leadership gifts were not so much discovered but uncovered as they faced challenging circumstances in a broken world. Their potential for impact was revealed as they stepped into uncharted territory in whatever way they hoped to build something different—for themselves, their families, their communities, and beyond.

My maternal grandmother grew up in Nigeria and lived to the rich age of one hundred and two before passing from this world to the next, leaving her legacy of a large, vibrant family. I never got the chance to meet her, but I gained glimpses of her personality through the stories my family told about her. I learned she was kind and strong. She was also a very determined businesswoman, going to the market every week to sell and trade in the community. I was told that when she reached the age of ninety-seven, my aunts and uncles actually had to persuade her to retire! Her husband, my grandfather, had passed away in the 1980s, so she'd been a widow for more than twenty years. Her resilience continued to carry her, even when death created a tomorrow that was unexpected.

My foster mother, Aunt May, lived in England through the tumultuous times of World War II. The pressure of war forced women into uncharted waters when they were called upon by the government to support the war effort. Because women were taking up roles previously occupied by men, their lives looked entirely different during the war. Women served in the armed forces, in agriculture, and in industry. They kept a nation moving during this dangerous period. When the Third Reich and its allies were defeated and the war was finally won, women shared in the victory (though it was decades before their contribution was given formal and public acknowledgment). Aunt May told me how much she hated modern-day films about women in that era. She felt it was romanticized, that their contribution was seen as frivolous. For her and her friends, it was anything but. What they did was in the bleak face of war, and it was work. They performed a vital service to their country.

When the war was over, women were thanked, but they were encouraged to return to their prewar lives and domestic roles. Hitler was dead, so it seemed that the grip of Nazism was extinguished (for the time being, at least). Men returning home from the war needed their jobs back.

But like any country affected by the devastation of war, the nation was not the same. It could never be. The men and the women were not the same. Including Aunt May. She had long decided she would never marry, so there was no plan for the typical domestic idyll for her. When the war effort was complete, drawing on her experiences looking after children evacuated from London, she decided to foster children. Who would have thought she'd find her life's purpose and vocation in the midst of war and tragedy? Or that she would be so influential in its aftermath?

Over the forty years that followed, she fostered more than a hundred children. I was one of the last to be fostered.[1] I like to think I was child number ninety-nine. When I came into her life, Aunt May was in her seventies, and like my grandmother, she, too, had to be persuaded to retire. Also like my grandmother, she passed away at the age of one hundred and two. Aunt May played her part in trying to fix a broken world during the war effort. Afterward, her life's mission was to nurture and raise the children who were wounded by it.

After the end of World War II and the attempt to resume prewar lives, it became clear that Britain had a significant labor shortage and needed immigration to boost the rebuild. The British Nationality Act of 1948 gave people from Commonwealth countries free entry to Britain,[2] so from the fifties and sixties onward, people from around the world responded to the invitation to work and rebuild. People traveled from the Caribbean, from India, and from countries in Africa, like Nigeria. And my family was among them. In the early sixties, my parents and others—who would become aunties and uncles—left Nigeria in pursuit of new adventures and opportunities.

They were young twentysomethings, visionaries in their own way, ready to build not only the nation but also new lives for themselves. Yet in spite of the law, immigrants were not always welcome. Sometimes they were deemed threats, seen as stealing jobs rather than contributing to the economy. Even though laws legislated against racial discrimination, it didn't stop it from happening. Therefore, these young immigrants gravitated toward people who understood them, who they felt safe around.

It was no wonder that as I grew older I was surrounded by a village of extended family members. Though not all of them were related by blood, they were fellow Nigerians (and some from the Caribbean) navigating a complex world together, understanding both one another's

roots and the British soil on which they were now planted. In one another's presence, they felt more known and understood, less lonely.
Isolation could leave them vulnerable.

A community was a source of both strength and support, just like
back home, just like living in a village. After all, everyday life needed
to continue. They needed to keep on going in and through the struggles. There was life to live, information to share about everything, such
as paying bills, finding material and a seamstress for when traditional
attire was needed, and where to buy hair products for Afro hair.

Furthermore, there was work to be done—fledgling careers to develop and retraining. There were resources to send to relatives overseas,
a next generation to birth and raise. Whatever obstacles, whatever opportunities the world threw at them, they would face them together—
and together achieve even more in the process.

Each generation of women discovered a path that led them to
uncover and utilize their gifts, to use their voices in unanticipated ways
in the world in which they lived. It was a path that led to opportunity,
even when it didn't look that way at first. It wasn't easy for any of them.
But when they engaged with the influence they now had, they made
an impact on their world.

Unlike my youngest daughter, I didn't have political ambitions at
age five. That year, Britain elected its first female prime minister, but I
couldn't make the same assumptions my daughter had. I didn't see
anyone who looked like me on Downing Street in the late 1970s and
early 1980s, so I was still dreaming of superheroes. My notions of influence and service, though sincere and heartfelt, were still deeply embedded in the realm of fantasy. Surely I could dream . . .

Like the women who came before me, I found it wasn't easy to uncover the path to living into my potential for influence. I attended an all-girls secondary school where the message was you could be whoever you wanted to be. The staff strove to empower the young women there. They cited the advancements women made in politics and culture and said there was no reason we couldn't do the same in the future. It was finally our time.

And though I was inspired, I also saw a society replete with contradictions. My teachers didn't live where I lived. Was it time for everyone, or *just* men and women like them, with their connections and opportunities? Those years were marked by an uneasy social and cultural climate. Did this exciting new landscape include women of every class? Poor women? Did it apply to immigrant women and their children? I wasn't so sure when I saw glimpses of tabloid newspapers in which pundits screeched about immigrants stealing English people's jobs.

Then came the tumult in my own life experiences with long-term foster care, as well as everyday occurrences like puberty in all its dramatic fullness that left me uncertain of my worth and value. I swung between feeling inspired and feeling insecure in the same hour.

I also could not ignore that in its own way, a path was being uncovered. I often say I was the last to know I had gifts, skills, and a contribution to make. That I already had influence. My self-doubt obscured the significance of indicators, such as leading initiatives at school, captaining the sports team, and participating in fundraising opportunities at church. I remember a teacher deliberately and specifically (and publicly) telling me I had a voice. Perhaps sensing I would misinterpret her words because I was in the school choir, she clarified by saying, "Joannah, I mean you have a *perspective,* something to say that matters, and a leadership role within your class." Though I appreciated her words, I couldn't receive their meaning. I couldn't own it.

It wasn't just my voice that was confusing me. As a Christian, I grew up hearing conflicting and contradictory and yet passionately held views on what a woman could and should be and what her area of influence was supposed to look like. By the time I reached college, sometimes those voices included very cute guys who had very strong opinions, who I was strongly drawn to for reasons *other* than their strong opinions.

The path leading toward influence, opportunity, and leadership began to open up through opportunities to work with the teenagers at my local church, then invitations to leadership roles and speaking opportunities on my college campus. *Something* was happening, but I still couldn't own it. I considered it something strange, even random, happening to me, even when I was enjoying the responsibility and opportunity.

I wasn't an influencer; I wasn't a leader. I was just someone who had strong opinions. People would sometimes wait for me to act upon shared opinions first and often sought my advice. *But I'm not a leader,* I reminded myself. *It just happens around me sometimes. I don't know why, but it's always been like this.*

In that era, I didn't see it as how God made me. I didn't see gifts. I didn't see influence. I didn't see that the path I was on was God-created, God-designed. I didn't see I was made for this. On a good day, I'd describe leadership as just the things I did. On a bad day, I saw it as a concession God made for a weird woman. And on a very bad day, I feared something was fundamentally wrong with me, that I wasn't woman enough.

That I was too much.

That I wanted the wrong things in life.

That I was the last person who should be given opportunity for influence.

I knew me. I knew that the brokenness of my past lingered in my life like a stale hangover. It left me with deep, quiet feelings of inadequacy that I worked hard to cover up—until I couldn't. I knew the cloud of sadness and pain would sometimes settle so heavily that I felt I was staring into an abyss. I also knew the vices I used to escape the way I felt. And knowing how quickly I swung between my insecurity and vanity, I also knew my ego and how I might feed it. Could I be trusted? *Should* I be trusted?

But sometimes I was inspired to make a difference in people's lives. Aunt May had. What if *I* could? I wanted to change the world, because where I grew up, it needed changing, needed investment. Yet at the same time, I felt disillusioned because I didn't see women who looked like me making an impact on their world. It was painfully rare in my environment. Some famous people loomed in the distance, and that was a blessing in its own way. But I needed to talk, to ask questions, to hear answers from women leaders. I needed to know how they wrestled with their own gifts and calls, or if they knew.

Battling with these things over many years felt lonely. If I really decided to commit to this path, wouldn't I just get lonelier? I knew how loneliness felt—palpably, physically—since childhood. I wouldn't choose that again. But surely I had to try to explore the stirrings inside me, the ideas in my head, and endeavor to put them to good use.

I kept moving forward because as I grew older, my faith was growing too. The more I encountered the power of Jesus in every fragment of my life, the more whole I became and the more I felt both grateful and compelled. I was grateful because Jesus was transforming me from the inside out—changing my perspective, healing my heart, challenging me. But I was compelled because knowing Him was life changing. I knew His good news was a life-giving, world-transforming change agent for the very fabric of society and all its systems and strata, as well as for the human heart.

> IF THERE WAS EVER A TIME TO *uncover* OUR POTENTIAL AND VOICES—IT'S NOW. NOW IS THE TIME TO BOLDLY AND AUTHENTICALLY REPRESENT GOD'S GOODNESS IN THE WORLD, LIVING AS CHANNELS FOR HIS TRANSFORMATIVE CHANGE AND *power*. NOW IS THE TIME TO RISE.

There was no one moment for me when I suddenly felt confident about having gifts worth using or influence that could make a positive impact on the world around me. Instead, I discovered over time that I was made for this. That it wasn't only in my blood, in my DNA, from the women who made me and raised me but it was in the design of the God who created me. Who, before anything went wrong with the world, created men and women in His image and likeness with a two-fold purpose: (1) to have a living and active relationship with Him and (2) to boldly represent Him in the world.

That kind of purpose is worth pushing past my fears for, because if there was ever a time to uncover our potential and voices—it's now.

Now is the time to boldly and authentically represent God's goodness in the world, living as channels for His transformative change and power.

Now is the time to rise.

CHANGING LANDSCAPES, SEISMIC SHIFTS, AND CULTURAL MOMENTS

We recently celebrated my mum's birthday at her favorite local restaurant. But as we drove around our old neighborhood, I was stunned by how much had changed. The grocery store and its parking lot had been replaced by stylish apartment blocks, and the huge flower market was about to be replaced by an embassy. New office buildings obscured the local library and my elementary school. The fish and chip shop no longer existed. The skyline, my skyline, was unrecognizable. Strangest of all, the roads were completely different from how they used to be, so I got lost and stuck in the neighborhood I'd lived in for most of my childhood and teenage years. Nothing was the same. It all seemed so sudden, so jarring.

In reality, our community had been changing for decades. The streets told a different story now. My mum had adjusted years ago, but I had to quickly recognize that the place I once knew was gone forever. I had to navigate "my" neighborhood in a new way.

We all find ourselves adjusting to new landscapes—not just the unexpected changing stories of our neighborhoods, but those of our personal lives. This could be a matriarch dealing with loss or ambitious young adults adjusting to life in a new country. Such upheaval can be chaotic and bewildering; it can also be transformative.

We also encounter seismic shifts in society that redefine the world we're living in. Some, like a global war, leave wide cracks and fault lines in the planet, affecting generations to come. Other moments, such as life-changing medical discoveries, feel like breakthroughs. The way we function in society has been transformed by technological advances, political movements, domestic terrorism, the rise or decline of faith in a community, and the demise of once-trusted institutions. All these changes produce a profoundly new cultural backdrop, an unrecognizable skyline. It can be frightening and painful in some instances, creative and innovative in others. But it's always disorienting, and it requires we learn how to navigate unexpected paths.

As women explore these uncharted paths, we're seeing more of their influence and leadership emerge as their voices, their stories, their contributions impact their world. This is not the first time, as women have been influencing history throughout time. Still, women are emerging in new, influential ways across the cultural landscape. We sense the shift as women activate grassroots movements and organize marches that mobilize their communities and inspire others to press for lasting social and cultural change. We hear it in the rise and strength and influence of the #MeToo and Time's Up movements, addressing long-ignored experiences of sexual assault and power abuses that have shattered women's lives. We note the shift through the leadership presence and influence of women in the political sphere and their pursuit of the highest levels of political office on the global stage.

In the US, the surge of women in the workforce in recent years has redefined the marketplace. According to the US Department of Labor report, women account for 47 percent of the workforce and own up to ten million businesses, resulting in $1.4 trillion in receipts. It was found that "mothers are the primary or sole earners for 40 percent of households with children under 18 today, compared with 11 percent in 1960."[3] The workforce is being reenvisioned as women's voices lead conversations about pay equality and parental leave.

Alongside this data are the conflicting journalistic think pieces debating a woman's place in society, how loud a woman's voice can be, whether it's loud enough. Voices ready to charge into a great unknown, facing off against voices who call for a return to a former, more familiar landscape—complete with its own distinct cultural expectations. The cacophony grows louder, but noise never stopped an earthquake; if anything, it might help intensify it. The skyline remains changed, and there are still new paths to explore.

It might be disorienting, but what if this were also an opportunity? What if our cultural moments uncovered a new path for our God-given design and call—a redeeming God who promised He would be doing a new thing and making all things new? Rather than being afraid of a shifting culture, we might discover new purpose there. That instead of hiding away in safe enclaves, we realize this is an opportunity to rise.

What if God gives us a vision for a new skyline? What if this were a window in time where we needed people to discover that their paths are bigger than themselves (and their own lives) and that they are invited to rise up and respond?

We need people who, rising into their influence, will demolish the institutionalization of ideologies that have broken communities and destroyed lives. We need people who will not only clear the rubble of old ideologies and mind-sets but also tend to those who have been broken and damaged by them. We need people who will uncover voices and gifts that respond to injustice, dehumanization, misogyny, racism, ableism, and every ism and phobia out there.

And we need people who will voice new dreams—new culture-shaping, community-healing, justice-and-mercy-living, potential-realizing, life-giving, God-inspired dreams. People who would be willing to play their parts and lead the way. Further still, we need to bring new ideas and see and act on the potential that a new land-scape can bring. We need to create new ways of being, of living and doing.

We're making our own chapter of history, and the world needs your faith-fueled voice, gifts, and skills. It needs you to rise into your God-given influence and make a positive impact. So you need to clear the debris and the obstacles standing in the way of unapologetically living the life you were made for. You'll need to dig deep to get there, and it might be a little uncomfortable at times, but it will be worth it.

Grace and peace to you as you continue in this book.

REVIEW AND REFLECT

Think of the women in your family tree—their stories and experiences. What limits and opportunities did they face, and how did they shape their lives and legacy?

Consider the limits and opportunities in your story. How have they shaped your life? How has your world changed in unexpected ways? Where has it been challenging? Where has it been transformative?

The Cost of Disempowerment

(And How I've Looked for Myself in All the Right Places)

Young girls need to see role models in whatever careers they may choose, just so they can picture themselves doing those jobs someday.

—SALLY RIDE

f only life were simple. If only we could simply clear away the obstacles and debris that stand in the way of our influence when life has shaken us to the core.

If only all that it took for women to live into the fullness of their influence and purpose was to simply decide that whatever happened before doesn't matter now. Or to hear "You can be all you want to be!" or "You're empowered; you go, girl!" to inspire a new way of living and breathing, as though all we needed was for an old day to end for the new one to begin. It's not that those words aren't meaningful or even in some way true; it's that those words are only pieces of the jigsaw puzzle. They do not build the complete picture; there are missing pieces.

To rise and engage with our purpose, we'll need to understand the impact of this changing world on our own stories. We'll need to get past the voices speaking at and over us about our potential for influence and hear God's call over our lives.

Years into my leadership—long past my adolescent angst and wonderings, with experience under my belt—there were still times, often months rather than fleeting moments here and there, when I struggled to be confident about my calling. I felt like a fake waiting to be found out. Even when I was (finally) convinced I had a voice and influence, I couldn't see a clear path for my growth and development. Instead, I felt as though I were stumbling around in the dark, trying to work it out. Besides, I'd never seen a woman *do it*—lead in the way and in the spaces that I was feeling called to lead. If I'd never seen a woman do it, was I trying to do something that simply couldn't be done?

So when my heart leaped to life and my mind buzzed with creative ideas and possibilities, fears caught up with me, warning me to tone myself down. When new opportunities that matched my skills and passions opened up, even when I was secretly thrilled, I *still* felt conflicted because I questioned if my excitement was an indicator of arrogance. Who did I think I was, anyway?

Some of the struggle was logistical. I was trying to work out how to raise children; be a wife, daughter, sister, friend, employee; and somehow still sleep and do laundry; all the while feeling that I wasn't managing anything or anyone well. I wanted to talk to someone. A woman who'd been there. Someone who could tell me how she did it and still managed to get some sleep. Not knowing who to talk to felt lonely.

My grandmother and Aunt May had passed before I knew the questions I wanted to ask them about this stage of my life. I had deep, soul-churning questions about womanhood, motherhood, how to handle work when life gets more painful and tragic, and what to do when the world spins out of control and life is turned on its head.

I wanted to ask them if they even felt like they were leading or if (as I suspect in Aunt May's case) life was happening so hard and fast that they were just getting on with it and didn't have time to reflect on what it "felt" like. I wanted to know how you take something valuable out of your trials and forge a new path. I wanted to know how you learn to lead people and family and life when you don't know where to start.

If you manage to overcome those doubts and insecurities and begin to believe you can lead, can you actually lead without second-guessing yourself at every turn? It felt as though there were so many questions and not enough places to go for insights and answers.

For years in my leadership journey, "You go, girl!" got up and went nowhere.

No, I could not do whatever I wanted to do.

No, I did not *have this*.

No matter how confident I looked on the outside, empowered was the last thing I was feeling on the inside. Instead, I felt perpetually uncertain and conflicted, inadequate with bursts of bravery—but mostly kind of tired.

Daring and courageous conversations with my male colleagues were often followed by my replaying conversations in my mind, feeling insecure about everything I said. *Did I say things in the right way? How did I come across? Was I too harsh? Will anyone think I'm bossy? Would anyone think a guy is bossy, or is he just a strong leader?*

I was passionate and hardworking (because everybody loves a worker bee, right?) but a bit (or a lot) closer to burnout than anyone should be comfortable with. Too often I'd feel hopeful, then frustrated, when I'd walk into a meeting and be the only woman there.

I was ill equipped for that, lacking mentoring and coaching for leadership in my skin, in my body, and in my womanhood. I longed for access to leaders who looked like me, who were further ahead on the journey, and whose living examples could help me.

Their absence had a debilitating and disempowering impact. It also slowed me down, made me question the validity of my dreams. Though ultimately it wasn't impossible to move forward, it was still very hard to find a way through, because as activist and educator Marian Wright Edelman said, "You can't be what you can't see."[1]

A Conversation, in Theory

We gathered a group of women. Just a few Christian women, leading and influencing in a range of spaces. Nonprofit leaders, entrepreneurs, corporate women, ministry leaders, pastors. Creatives. We met because I had invited them to a meal, a chance to gather and meet with other women leaders. And talk. Just talk.

Each replied to me with one part openness, one part weariness, a dose of jadedness, a side of suspicion, and yet cautious optimism as well. They had just enough curiosity to attend at least once.

We met in a private room in a restaurant, merely a modest side room with a large round table with place settings. At the dinner were Bree, Rachel, Kate, CeCe, Angela, and Amber. A large white envelope sat in the center of the table. A server bustled about, bringing water and taking orders. Although the women were essentially strangers, it didn't take long for conversation to flow past brief introductions and pleasantries to their shared curiosity about my invitation.

Kate started: "I was curious because I knew who some of you were, and I'd meant to reach out. But you know what it's like—it never happens."

Rachel shared, "The free meal sealed the deal for me! It meant I didn't need to cook tonight."

"I was concerned it was going to be another Bible study," confessed Bree. "I'm the women's director at a local church, so it's not that I'm not interested in Bible studies. It's just that I go to a lot of those; I prepare a lot of those. I don't really have time for one more."

She paused, remembering these women didn't know her well. "I'm not saying I'm looking for more than the Bible, you understand," she said hurriedly. "I'm just looking after all these people, hearing all their stories, and I need . . ."

Amber smiled and placed her hand on Bree's. "Look around the table. I think we all get it. You don't have to explain yourself here."

I watched them all assessing their fellow women leaders. Different leadership contexts, for sure. They didn't all have the same ethnic background, age, marital status, stories, or histories, but they were women and they were leaders. Would they be safe with one another? Did they even know they were meant to be at this dinner? I could see the insecurity, and I suspected they'd give voice to it.

Would they give this conversation a chance? I knew that part was up to each individual woman.

Bree exhaled and continued: "I just need more, you know? Is it bad to say that? I need something that will develop not just my knowledge but my skill in leading. I need more than information and input. I need to process sometimes, and I need to know *how*—how to lead, how to apply all the great input I get. Our Bible studies aren't built for that. They are built for many other wonderful things. They show me who God is. They remind me of the principles I live and, yes, that I lead by. But they don't teach me *how* to put those principles into practice as a leader. They don't tell me how to develop into the best leader I can be for the women I love and serve."

She glanced around the circle. "These are people's lives I'm dealing with here. I cannot mess this up. And the truth is, I don't even know if I'm doing a good job, and I don't know how to grow as a leader. When my male colleagues were at seminary training to be pastors, I was at home with my kids. I didn't even expect to lead. That wasn't my plan A, my plan B, or anything. It wasn't my plan! I didn't ask for this. But now people come to me to talk about their marriages, their crises. They tell me stories and secrets they've never told anyone before. I'm still not entirely sure how I got here. But I'm here now. And here isn't going away."

I watched as Bree looked down at her hand, which Amber had grasped while Bree was speaking. Amber continued to hold it, smiling and nodding at her.

"Yep," Amber said, clearing her throat. "Like I said, we get it."

A few other women murmured in agreement around the table, and I decided it was time to introduce the topic of discussion. I read off a card, "*Disempower.* The definition, per Merriam-Webster, is 'to deprive of power, authority, or influence: make weak, ineffectual, or unimportant.'[2] And the question I'd like to pose to you all is, What does disempowerment look like in practice, in the real world?"

"Okay, let's go straight there," said Kate. "I guess if you're going to talk about empowering women, it's worth thinking through the things that disempower us. Anyone have thoughts?"

"Jobs where the buck kind of stops with you but the decisions stop with someone else," said CeCe. "I remember my first job was like that. I worked hard—still do! And so because of that, I was always given more responsibilities and frequently asked if I could 'just do this' or 'just do that.' They'd say things like, 'You're so capable, it'll take you no time,' as they left a pile of things on my desk. I was trying hard to be seen as leadership potential at work, so I did it all."

Angela groaned. "Nooo . . ."

"Right? You know where this is going, don't you? I know too—now. And every time I had an idea to make the processes better, to make a decision to bring about change, I was ignored or shut down. Eventually my boss called me into her office. She told me I was stepping beyond my boundaries and then reminded me of my specific job duties. No one minded when I was helping them out, backing them up, doing their research, or solving the crisis. But when it came to having any actual authority—the permission or place to effect change or make improvements—then apparently I was controlling. I was tired of the dynamic, and I felt devalued. So I left."

The women around the table seemed to collectively exhale. Then Bree said, "I feel I need to qualify the things I'm about to say because I'm afraid you're going to think I hate men. I don't. I love my husband. I love my sons. I love my brothers, my dad. I've got great colleagues who are guys. Yet it feels like work largely operates in a world built for men. The networking opportunities are over a game or drinks. I love football, but I feel weird if I'm the only woman there. But they are talking, connecting, getting ahead, and I have to turn down those opportunities to network because they don't fit my life. I want to spend time with my boys after work. I want to watch their games. I've got a car pool to do, mealtimes, bedtime routines. Where's the time to watch a game just to 'connect'? Does that sound bad?"

"No," Rachel answered. "I think you make a great point. It's problematic to assume that just because we're critiquing processes that don't work, we think less of men or think they shouldn't be in their jobs. We just want to be there too, working to our full potential, alongside them. And it's not just the net-working we're missing out on. It's the golf-course mentoring, the informal leadership development that happens in those environ-ments, when everyone is a bit more relaxed. That's the moment when they spot potential, that the bosses see Craig or Steve in a new light. And again, I am not there, because I cannot be. My very presence there would change the dynamic. I'm not 'one of the boys' and never will be, and I'm beginning to resent it, but I'm trying not to resent *them.* I'm missing out on something simply because they don't see me."

Amber spoke up. "Disempowerment looks like being unseen and uninvited to the table where decisions are made. Disempow-erment looks like not being expected or encouraged to make significant contributions to areas like policy that shape the cul-ture of the workplace. When the decisions and policies don't recognize the lives we women actually lead. That we are working mothers, working caregivers. And that we are committed to our *whole* lives. Maybe the reason the men are free to go for it is because their 'team' is holding it down at home. And good for them! But how many teams can I be on at once? I'll be out of fingers and toes to count on!"

The women laughed. Then Angela said, "Seriously, though. The people at the top of any organization determine the culture of it, what the acceptable behavior is. They shape the language. Terms like *casting couch* instead of *sexual coercion* or *rape*? Or *locker room talk* instead of *harassment* or *misogyny.* Leaders define the tone and feel of a place. What the leader values, everybody values, whether you like it or not. And a culture can make or break a leader, male or female.

"When I was starting out, I had a job at a place where women were objectified. How we dressed mattered, and it mattered that our clothing was form fitting, but not too fitting, you know, because if your clothes fit too snugly, that made you slutty. It was okay to make demeaning, belittling, patronizing, or sexual comments, but to complain was to be 'overly sensitive' because 'it was just a bit of fun.' Someone even said once, 'I thought you'd appreciate the attention.' I'm trying to do my job, and I'm supposed to be grateful for harassment?"

Angela shook her head. "A good number of men have led differently, and I'm grateful for them and how they have empowered me. But I think it would change my life to see women leading at the top of their games, shaping and creating healthy cultures for everyone."

Rachel chimed in. "It's disempowering when you don't see other women doing *it*—leading in the same position you have or leading in the roles you hope to have one day. It makes you question if you can."

CeCe added, "Or if you should. When I don't see people who look like me, I wonder if there is a place for me, if I am welcome or will be valued."

Bree put up her hand as if asking permission. "Can I ask you, and forgive me if I sound clumsy or use the wrong words, but CeCe, Rachel, Amber, do you ever feel it on a cultural level too?"

"Always," CeCe answered. "Every time I walk in the room, I think, *Am I welcome? A black woman here? Is my voice, my experience, the cultural lenses—are they welcome? Can I bring my whole self here?* And the truth is, not always, and it's tiring."

"Sometimes you're dealing with assumptions made about you culturally," Rachel said. "I have felt I'm 'off code' for what some people from majority culture seem to expect of an Asian American woman. I don't fit their expectation. Aside from being hurt by the cultural stereotypes, I feel the person I actually *am* is dismissed. It feels like rejection."

It seemed like it was time for me to ask a follow-up question. "What do you think this disempowerment is costing us? We know what it's cost us personally. It's cost us our confidence, our courage. That is certain. But what else?"

Amber spoke. "Maybe there are jobs we've stayed in too long or opportunities we didn't go for because we were afraid. I thought it was just me, you know? I thought this was my problem, that I was the problem. With you guys, here tonight, I'm not the only one who has felt this. So I'm wondering, beyond this table, what has this collective disempowering—whether intentional or not—done to our families, our schools, our cities, even our culture?

"We're all leaders, influencers, or whatever the word is we use these days. But we're also believers, and the roles we have, the jobs or projects we're doing, are informed by our faith. We're here, but we've all felt disillusioned and lonely and that we wanted to give up. And sometimes we did."

The conversation continued, each woman sharing her experiences. They spoke of the people who believed in them and gave them opportunities. They spoke of times they were overlooked and what it cost them.

I believe that upon leaving the restaurant, each woman felt that the evening was better than expected and more meaningful, more honest than she had hoped when walking in—just being in the room with other women who were asking questions about their purpose and leadership. Just a space where they could answer in the way they wanted to, even if their statements couldn't be tied in a neat and tidy bow. They all felt less alone, even though until that meal, they hadn't realized that the grinding feeling they had gotten used to over the years was loneliness, a sense of isolation. And I believed that even if they didn't know where our group could go together, they were willing to find out.

Purpose Unfulfilled?

Disempowerment is not every woman's experience, nor is leadership and influence every woman's desire. Yet when any human being, male or female, is denied the opportunity to realize his or her God-given potential and make the contribution to society he or she was designed to make, we all miss out on the impact that person could make on the world.

We need the voices and influence of healthy, empowered women to make an impact on our world for the common good. It's not a radical new idea; development agencies serving countries across the globe have long acknowledged the powerful role women and girls play in rebuilding societies and communities around the world.

Kofi Annan, the seventh secretary general of the United Nations and Nobel Peace Prize winner, noted, "There is no tool for development more effective than the empowerment of women."[3] However, it's not just true of women in countries described by the West as "the developing world" or "emerging economies." It's true of women in every stratum of every community of every country on earth. Global research of the business world reveals that including women in leadership improves a business's bottom line, as does ethnic diversity.[4]

WE NEED THE VOICES AND *influence*
OF HEALTHY, EMPOWERED WOMEN
TO MAKE AN IMPACT ON OUR
WORLD FOR THE *common* GOOD.

A study showed that when a company had 30 percent female leadership, its net margin increased by up to six percentage points.[5] Other research found that 20 percent female leadership at "decision-making level" in a company resulted in that company's higher performance.[6] Yet research also indicated that though men and women are equal when it comes to demonstrated managerial skills, underlying cultural bias in the workplace and in culture at large means women are not perceived equally and do not get equal opportunity to take executive positions.[7] Women currently make up only 6.4 percent of CEOs of Fortune 500 companies.[8] What are we missing in their absence, not only in business but wherever their potential might be realized?

What is the cost when a woman lacks access and investment, encouragement to own her voice, and opportunities for influence in her sphere when there is no obvious pathway to progress?

Start-up companies that never start
Nonprofits that are not birthed into our communities
Churches that aren't planted
Songs and books and art that are left unwritten/uncreated
Risks that aren't taken
Neighborhoods that are not nurtured and connected
Families of every shape and size that are not strengthened
Scientific discoveries that are left unknown

It's not just about the bad news when women don't get to be all they were designed to be. It's the absence of the good news for human flourishing that matters too.

Thank God Someone stepped onto the stage of human history and modeled a different way for all of us to learn from and live by.

Thank God we follow a Man who has called women into this moment and told them this is what they are made for. He invited them into a new way of living and leading and continues to extend the invitation today.

REVIEW AND REFLECT

What has disempowerment looked like in your life?

What dreams and ideas have you put on hold because you didn't know how to get there?

Talitha Koum!

(And What Jesus Really Says About Women)

"It's gonna hurt, now," said Amy. "Anything dead coming back to life hurts."

—Toni Morrison

When I met Jesus and became a Christian at nine years old, I was introduced to Him as God, my savior and friend, and I loved Him with all the fervency and devotion my young heart and mind could muster. Though there were huge parts of my faith that were vast and broken unknowns (it would take years to even begin to comprehend that God was also a heavenly Father), I was fascinated by Him and excited to follow Him.[1]

The Jesus I was introduced to was not distant and theoretical. My Sunday school teachers taught us that Jesus was active throughout history and that He was moving in and around the world today. It was in Sunday school that I learned about women like Mary Slessor, a missionary to Calabar, Nigeria. I learned about Corrie ten Boom and the power of forgiveness expressed to those who brutalized her and her sister and many others in concentration camps during World War II. I heard about missionary Jackie Pullinger leaving England to serve in Hong Kong. I learned about Christians in different countries who were living for Christ in extraordinary ways.[2] Each story felt like an expectation and invitation to be part of what God was doing in the world. Jesus changed people and places. Jesus changed the world. Jesus was good for the world.

Granted, I was only nine years old at the time; but even though I didn't understand the world around me through an adult lens, I wasn't too young to experience the world and believe that things should be different. I wasn't too young to experience a broken home and the absence of relationships, to experience racism and sexism, to intuitively feel the brunt and inequity of stereotypes in our community and country. Furthermore, I wasn't too young to be bullied at school or feel sad, or too young to believe in Jesus or believe in hope and change. He was moving around the world, so when would it happen here?

Then adolescence swept me away on a detour where other things like boys, clothes, and friends became far more important issues. The stories of Jesus working in the world faded from view, and His significance faded from my values. My faith was still there. After all,

I couldn't argue with the encounters I'd had with Him. Jesus was still my savior. On a Sunday. But everything else that was important to me—like acceptance, and, let's be honest, popularity and a hot body—was far more pressing. And though I was already beginning to uncover and wrestle with my potential and talents and place in the world, I hadn't thought of God's role or voice in that.

I met Jesus again at age eighteen. It started one summery evening. The gorgeous swaths of blue, red, and gold of the sunset are still so vivid in my mind that the memory of it brings tears to my eyes to this day. It was this marvel of creation that lit my pathway home from work, and it took my breath away because it reminded me of a friend (and savior) I hadn't really talked to in such a long time because I thought I was so grown up and mature. I missed Him.

Our conversations in the years and decades to come were very different from those of my childhood faith. Some things remained. Jesus was still my savior and the King—the friend I had met when I was nine years old.

And He was still a revolutionary, changing the world, inviting me to join Him in what He was doing, to participate in the stories He was creating in the world. I shouldn't have been surprised by the ways He was changing the world, of course. I'd read the Bible and saw that when Jesus came to earth, He revolutionized people's understanding of the human condition, life, and love; He was an earthquake to humanity's understanding of what it meant to know God and be known by Him; and He radically redefined our value and purpose, and began a movement of followers that brought transformation to the role of women in society. A brand-new day.

OLD TESTAMENT FOUNDATIONS, NEW TESTAMENT TRANSFORMATION

It would be unfair and inaccurate to suggest that only after Jesus arrived did women uncover a path, purpose, and influence in their walk with God. Even in the Old Testament, we see women who left legacies after leading impactful lives. They were married, single, wealthy, poor, respected, unknown. Regardless, in God's hands, they had transforming influence. We think of Hagar, the enslaved African woman whose revelation and encounter with God shapes theology to this day with the phrase *El Roi,* which means "You are the God who sees me" (Genesis 16:13). Or Miriam, a prophetess and worshipper who led with Moses and Aaron (see Micah 6:4) and was likely the most influential woman among God's people during the days of the Exodus. There's Deborah, the judge who called God's people to rise against oppression (see Judges 4–5); Esther, a queen who advocated for the survival of God's people (see the book of Esther); and less talked about figures such as Huldah (see 2 Kings 22:14–20), an adviser to the king. The defining culture did not have the last word on women's influence.[3]

Although in the Old Testament we more often see special and unique individuals, men and women appointed and empowered by God for His purposes, the reset Jesus brings means everyone—including women—is invited and included in God's mission to change the world.

The late New Testament scholar David Scholer remarked,

As a Jewish male in an androcentric [male-centered], patriarchal society, Jesus' respect for women as persons of dignity and worth and his inclusion of them as disciples and proclaimers in his life and ministry was very significant in its own first-century context for women and their place and activity in ministry in the earliest churches and is important as a heritage for both Jewish and Christian people today.[4]

When we look directly at the life, death, and resurrection of Jesus, we see how He *saw* women. He redefined how culture understood every woman's potential, and He modeled it for His community, in His community, and through His community. Author Michele Guinness wrote, "Jesus doesn't only raise the status of women. He raises the status of all human beings by showing them what God intended them to be."[5]

Jesus saw women, their worth and their value, even when they were unseen by others.

The gospel writers tell the story of a woman who'd been subject to bleeding for twelve years. Attempts at treating her condition had resulted in nothing more than her poverty, and her condition rendered her an outcast in her culture. Desperate for hope and healing, the woman took a risk—she made her way through the crowds pressing against Jesus, with the goal of touching His cloak so that she might be healed. The risk paid off, because when she touched Jesus, the bleeding stopped. But before she had a chance to leave, Jesus asked who had touched Him. In front of the crowd, she told her story. Jesus responded, "Daughter, your faith has healed you. Go in peace" (Luke 8:48). She was no longer an outcast, she was healed, and she was whole. Instead of being defined by her condition, her faith was affirmed by Jesus. She was restored to her place in the community.

Jesus then continued on His journey to heal the daughter of Jairus, the synagogue leader. Someone from Jairus's household brought news of the twelve-year-old's death and (understandably) said there was no reason for Jesus to visit anymore. Jesus insisted, went to their home, took the girl's hand, and said, *"Talitha koum!"*—"Little girl, I say to you, get up!" (Mark 5:41)—and raised her from the dead.

Jesus saw and affirmed women at their most broken and vulnerable, and He didn't do it at a distance, nor did He treat them as emotionally, intellectually, or theologically deficient, fragile creatures. Jesus engaged with women and entered robust theological discussion, talking about the nature of worship with a *Samaritan* woman in an era in which such was the enmity between the groups that there even existed a Jewish proverb that said, "The daughters of the Samaritans are menstruants from the cradle."[6]

When Mary stepped beyond the cultural norms of her day, leaving Martha to attend to domestic duties and hospitality in order to sit and learn from Jesus, He acknowledged Martha's frustration but affirmed Mary's decision. We often use this story to contemplate our need for rest and to highlight the priority of our devotional lives above our busyness. Still, Mary's posture was more than devotional. Women were educated in the Scriptures, but sitting at the feet of a rabbi for theological instruction said a lot more than devotion. To listen to the rabbi for theological instruction reflected a desire to become and live like the rabbi. As such, it was seen as a job for men.[7] Not any longer. Jesus said to Martha in the presence of His accompanying disciples that "Mary has chosen what is better, and it will not be taken away from her" (Luke 10:42).

Perhaps most striking is that Jesus included women in His mission. In Luke 8, we meet Joanna, Susanna, and Mary—all women who traveled with Jesus and the twelve and supported them out of their own means (see verses 2–3). According to Scholer, these women were more than sponsors. The word used (and its compounds) to describe their following Jesus occurs more than seventy-five times in the Gospels and generally means "being a disciple."[8]

Then there's the Resurrection itself, that earth-shattering, game-changing, all-things-made-new moment in history. Despite knowing that a woman's words were not even accepted in a court of law, Jesus chose women to make the proclamation of this amazing news.

> PERHAPS IT IS NO *wonder* THAT THE WOMEN WERE FIRST AT THE CRADLE AND LAST AT THE CROSS. THEY HAD NEVER *known* A MAN LIKE THIS MAN—THERE NEVER HAS BEEN SUCH ANOTHER.
>
> —Dorothy Sayers

What must it have been like for these women to follow Jesus? He had a vision and purpose for their lives that was radically different from the world they'd grown up in. A little girl would rise to new life, and an outcast seen as unclean would be healed, publicly affirmed, and restored. A woman would learn from a rabbi alongside the men and travel with Him and His team. A Samaritan woman would have something to say that could change her community for the better. A group of women would be entrusted with the message of the Resurrection.

Newly commissioned by the risen Jesus, the early church followed in His footsteps and His gospel mission. Both men and women served and led in a range of capacities, living for the gospel at considerable risk to themselves at times, some dying for their faith. The women following and serving Jesus, as well as their spheres of influence, did not fit a single, specific mold. Lydia was a successful businesswoman with a large home and household who came to faith through Paul's ministry (see Acts 16:11–15). By persuading Paul and his team to stay at her house, Lydia played an instrumental role in the flourishing church and community in Philippi and in bringing the gospel to a new continent: Europe. Eunice and Lois were a mother and grandmother respectively, who, according to Paul, played significant roles in forming Timothy (see 2 Timothy 1:5), who would go on to become one of the key future leaders of the church. There were prominent church leaders like Priscilla, who taught Apollos (see Acts 18:24–28), and Phoebe, who served as a deacon and patron with considerable influence in Cenchreae (see Romans 16:1–2). The known world and culture was transformed by these women's voices, influence, and impact.[9]

STEPPING INTO UNCHARTED TERRITORY

I'm curious what it must have been like for the women in the Gospels to respond to Jesus's call and mission. What must it have felt like for Mary to stay in the room and learn from Jesus when she was expected to sit elsewhere? Was it vulnerable or awkward for Joanna, Susanna, and Mary to travel with Jesus as part of His team, no longer defined by their pasts but fully committed to His present and future mission?

Then later, did it take all their courage to proclaim Jesus's resurrection, the most important news in the world, knowing their voices weren't validated or taken seriously by law?

Jesus redefined their lives, values, identities, and mission. He also redefined their community and the world they lived in.

When the women were commissioned (alongside the men!) and the early church began, they were launched into the great unknown. There were no road maps or GPS for the journey they were now exploring. I can't help but wonder how long it took Lydia to persuade Paul and his team to stay at her home and how her offer might have been perceived. Wider society was sometimes enthralled by the church, and at others time they brutally persecuted the believers, women included. Even so, the gospel still spread across the known world, and some historians note that Christianity was particularly popular among women in the early life of the church because women in the church were often afforded higher status and opportunity than in their wider communities.[10] Wouldn't it be amazing if the church could someday be known once again as being particularly compelling to women because it was a place of value, affirmation, and empowerment—just like Jesus?

Still, who could possibly be the mentors and guides as the first generation of women in the church? Who could help them navigate what it meant to live fully and freely as commissioned and called women in a world that didn't always see their potential? To explore life in Christ in the face of old stories and cultural mores? At least the old way was familiar. But now the pathway was not only unfamiliar but unprecedented. A brand-new path was unfolding with every step they took. The women had one another and a group of men all exploring this new life together. Yet they all (men and women) had a transformational, compelling relationship with Jesus. They were empowered by Him and given gifts from Him, commissioned into the world by Him. Through their relationship with Him, Jesus illuminated the pathway as they walked into the unknown.

Two thousand years later, Jesus is still moving. We serve a God who fully sees us, loves us, and meets us where we are. He is a savior who walks where we've walked and touches our lives with His power, and He transforms the most broken and bloodied parts of our stories with His resurrective power. Jesus is a savior, friend, king, and liberator—and a man like no other before or since. But as wonderful as that is, it doesn't end with our own individualized, personalized transformation package. After all, as filmmaker Ava DuVernay said, "If your dream only includes you, it's too small."[11]

To follow Jesus leads to more, because Jesus's final words to His followers on earth were a commission to His disciples, a command to play our part in His Great Commission and make disciples of all peoples. To follow One who is making all things new. It's a commission to represent Him in a world shifting too fast for humans to handle, a commission to invest all the gifts, abilities, and talents He's given to influence the world *for* good. It's not a radical, culturally palatable premise for women, nor a way for the church to keep up with the changing face of society. No, women living into their God-given influence is very old good news. It's as old as the Gospels, as old as Old Testament figures such as Deborah, and as old as an ancient garden called Eden.

He's inviting you.

He's calling you.

He has already commissioned you.

And He's waiting for your response.

(LITTLE) GIRL, RISE UP!

Like those of the women of the New Testament, our paths are likely complicated and unclear. Perhaps they are paths we didn't anticipate or paths we can't see because they're covered by our broken or painful backstories.

Perhaps we exist in spaces where our voices are not heard or taken seriously. Maybe they don't see us at all. Perhaps our context has been so disempowering that it's the norm for our lives.

> YOU HAVE A *life-changing*, CULTURE-SHAPING, HEAVEN-TOUCHING-EARTH TYPE OF INFLUENCE. YOU HAVE A COMMISSION TO FULFILL.

Maybe the challenge lies elsewhere. We know we have influence and the opportunities to shape our world, but we're the first or one of few women in our environment. So we're all making it up as we go, whatever our life stage (married, single, empty-nester, busy mom), pioneering new policies and practices as we enter them. It's new and invigorating, and we're uncertain if we are doing the right thing. It would be great to have someone ahead of us showing us how to make it all work.

Yet we follow a God who illuminates our pathways, complications and all, as we try to step into the unknown. Even though we've given up and people around us have given up on us, He takes us by the hand and invites us to rise up with the life and strength that only He can give us.

You have a life-changing, culture-shaping, heaven-touching-earth type of influence. You have a commission to fulfill.

Whoever you are:

Your potential is worth cultivating.

Your God-given dreams need exploring.

Your talents and gifts need affirming and developing.

Your voice needs to be heard.

Your call needs to be responded to.

Your part in the Great Commission needs to be fulfilled.

Your influence needs to be unlocked.

Your impact needs to be felt.

You are worth investing in.

So it's time to rise up.

REVIEW AND REFLECT

Which women in the Bible inspire you and why?

Identify your areas of influence (for example: family, profession, volunteer roles, local community). Imagine Jesus inviting you to rise up in those places and step into your influence. What could that look like?

The Surprising Answer to "What Would Jesus Do?"

(And Why Pedicures Are Not Required)

In order to rise, you have to lay your burden down.

—Sally Helgesen and
Marshall Goldsmith

It was Passover in Jerusalem, the time when the people of God remembered and celebrated a great deliverance: when the Israelites were set free from slavery. Yet now God's people were oppressed again, this time under the sophisticated imperial might of the Roman Empire. Nonetheless, the people traveled from across the region to the city to celebrate, to remember, to hope (or perhaps mourn), all the while not knowing God was walking through their streets, healing people, transforming lives, and weeping over their city, preparing for a greater deliverance to come. The presence of travelers swelled the city to an estimated one million people.

While the city was electrified with the dynamic of more people, it had its downside. There were more people (and their livestock) to walk among—to step on and be stepped on *by*. More people meant more heat and sweat, more dust and dirt to walk through, more waste and animal filth to step in. And because the shoes that people of this time wore were open toed, just a thin strap to secure the sole in place, nobody could escape the downside.

When hosting people for a meal at one's home, it was customary to wash the guests' feet as a generous act of hospitality. Cleansed of the dirt, dust, filth, and sweat, the guest was renewed, and everyone could enjoy the evening without invasive street odors.

Cleaning feet was, understandably, considered a disgusting task. During Passover, it would only be worse. Foot washing was seen as so lowly that rabbinic law stated that disciples didn't have to do this for their rabbis. So low that even a Jewish male slave didn't have to do it. It was a task reserved for those who were seen to be the least significant in society: women, children, foreigners, and the marginalized.

So when a popular young rabbi—known for incredible wisdom, for healing the sick, for casting out demons, and for confronting the religious powers of the day—wrapped a towel around His waist and picked up a basin of water, it was more than unusual. It was unthinkable. It was an outrageous, unimaginable act.

There are many rich insights to gain from this moment in John 13 when Jesus washed His disciples' feet. Some theologians emphasize the power of His humble act of service. Some see this moment as a symbol of baptism. Others remind us of the lasting, profound significance when Jesus is in the room, identifying with the marginalized in society. Others recognize that the language in the text here of Jesus taking off His clothing and taking up garments is unusual and see this passage specifically symbolizing Jesus's crucifixion. Alongside all these insights and more, this passage captures a glimpse of Jesus, the leader, responding to the needs of the people He's spent three years investing in. Within hours, Jesus will be arrested, interrogated, tortured, and killed. These people will, within mere days and weeks, undertake the leadership of a movement that none of them expected. And none of them would say they were prepared for the journey ahead.

This evening captures many of Jesus's last words to His disciples, and even though they don't know it, Jesus does. There is not much time left, so His words and actions to His emerging leaders carry an extra weight and poignancy.

In this room, where the disciples had been arguing about who was the greatest among them, Jesus rises to His feet.

Would He teach? Would He prophesy? He speaks in a way no other religious leader could. He speaks with authority.

But He says nothing. The young rabbi just takes off His outer garments and puts them to one side. He motions for the towel in the corner, and when it's passed to Him, He wraps it around His waist.

The disciples glance at one another, confused. It wasn't that Jesus was about to do something unusual. The unusual had become normal with Jesus. They'd come to expect the unexpected: a healing, a message that would blow people's minds, a challenge to the religious leaders whose condemning words had shamed them all for so long.

But what now? Foot washing—so obvious but so unlikely, *so implausible* it doesn't even enter their minds.

It is only when Jesus slowly fills the basin with water that it begins to dawn on them. Then He gets on His knees in front of His disciples. Turning to them, Jesus smiles and asks, "Would you take off your sandals? Can I wash your feet?"

This was Jesus—healer, rabbi, Messiah, the one who would deliver God's people. *Why is He adopting such a lowly position in the room? What is He saying by identifying with the lowest of the low?*

Beyond the big "Why are You doing this, Jesus?" questions, I think of how self-conscious each disciple would have been on a personal level as Jesus moved toward them. How aware they are of the smell of their feet. How they reacted as He holds each foot, cleans in between each toe, touches the ingrained dirt, the traces of animal filth, and wipes them clean. The sudden flinch anytime Jesus touches and cleanses a cut or open wound. I think about how it must have felt at a visceral level and how vulnerable they probably were in that moment and then how Peter has a way of interrupting:

> When Jesus got to Simon Peter, he objected and said, "I can't let you wash my dirty feet—you're my Lord!"
>
> Jesus replied, "You don't understand yet the meaning of what I'm doing, but soon it will be clear to you."
>
> Peter looked at Jesus and said, "You'll never wash my dirty feet—never!"

"But Peter, if you don't allow me to wash your feet," Jesus responded, "then you will not be able to share life with me." (John 13:6–8, TPT)

Jesus explains to Peter that this moment was an integral part of life with Him, not an optional extra. Peter wants as much of Jesus's life as he can have, so finally he relents.

When Jesus completes the task, He instructs all His disciples to do the same for one another. The fact that John recorded this story in his gospel is an indicator that this moment was unforgettable.

They saw another feature of the nature of Jesus, indeed—of the nature of God in the moment: That as they lived and led and walked through the messy, broken world they sought to change, their deliverer was close by, closer than they'd imagined. And that He went to them and got down to where they were and washed their feet. He tended to their wounds, washed off the dust and the dirt, washed the sweaty weariness. He saw where they'd been and how it had affected them. He touched them, healed them, restored them, and refreshed them for the journey ahead.

They didn't encounter a distant, exacting leader who simply expected them to get out there and get the job done, regardless of where they were in their lives. They encountered Jesus who, knowing He was entrusting the future of His ministry—with all its opportunities and challenges—to these disciples, met them first, met their needs, and accepted who they were. The conversations about the future and the leadership tasks ahead would come. But on this evening, Jesus made a priority of connecting with them and investing in their well-being. He washed their feet.

———

As we walk through life and leadership in our world, it's inevitable that we're affected by it. Even though Jesus was and is radically counter-cultural in His treatment and commissioning of women, it's still hard to rise up into the commission He's given us when we're weighed down by the burden of the journey. The journey wearies us because it's costly when the systems and powers in our culture limit our potential and opportunities. Some of us had to work longer hours to prove our value and contribution. Others of us expended mental and emotional energy ensuring that our strength wasn't seen as threatening or bitchy. Or we overanalyzed what we could and should wear. It's tiring, and it leaves us longing for deliverance.

Sometimes the path feels like an uphill struggle and wears us out. Or it's just long and tiring as we carry our baggage and responsibilities with us. There are other occasions on our journeys when we stumble in our lives and leadership and we're left wounded and bleeding. In the hustle of human interaction and competitive careers, we're pushed out of the way, pushed down, and we're deeply wounded by someone else's selfishness or cruelty or ignorance. Words that cannot be unsaid get under our skin and cut at our hearts.

It's hard to keep walking when we are wounded and bleeding. We limp through our nights, begging for the panic, fear, and sleeplessness to stop, but stumble through our days, trying to act as though nothing is wrong or at least as though we are coping. But in reality, we bring our bleeding and oozing into our lives, relationships, potential, and leadership.

Aside from the external challenges that have an effect on our paths, there are also internal ones. We're still only human, with quirks and weaknesses and unhealthy traits and motives that influence us. We have patterns of thinking and acting, propensities and tendencies we're not proud of.

Life and leadership are so hectic and full that it's easy to lose focus and feel drawn to things that have a detrimental impact on us. Some of our weaknesses even start as strengths, but then our exercise habits become addictive or we use food or drink or entertainment or relationships to numb our feelings and mask our wounds. Our love for people turns into doing or even overdoing things because we need to be needed. Our healthy work ethic becomes workaholism in every sphere of our lives, and it's easier to not feel anything that way. We need help with our weaknesses before they become defining obstacles across our paths.

> THE LORD IS *close* TO THE BROKEN-
> HEARTED AND SAVES THOSE WHO
> ARE CRUSHED IN *spirit*.
> —Psalm 34:18

How do you walk into your leadership carrying the heavy baggage of both your burdens and your everyday responsibilities?

How do you live with the wounds and the weariness? How do you live with the vulnerability of your weaknesses?

Jesus left His prominent position to wash His disciples' feet before

He commissioned them on an uncharted leadership path. And similarly, He left the splendor of heaven to reach down to us and meet us where we are before commissioning us onward.

We need Jesus to wash our feet.

Our weary, sweaty feet.

Our wounded, bleeding feet.

Our weak and bruised feet.

What we need reaches beyond having a "come to Jesus" moment. We need to discover that Jesus already sees us and comes close to us to wash our feet.

Will you let Him?

Or instead, like Peter, do you push back and say, "I can't let You do this; it's not supposed to be this way; I'd never let You wash my feet"?

We might not say it as directly as Peter, but we can be just as obstinate. Instead, our way of pushing back is to not bring our wounds to Jesus for healing. We'll bring our tasks for only blessing, approval, and success. We'll discuss and debate with our peers who's doing best among us. It's as though we believe that all God is interested in is all we do for Him, our positions and progress, our roles and responsibilities. Yet in His interactions with leaders in the Gospels, Jesus consistently demonstrates that He is far more interested in people's characters than in their gifts, titles, connections, and achievements. It is still true today.

Perhaps we're too ashamed—after all, we're supposed to be leaders, influencers, the ones getting it right.

> How can we bring that eating disorder (that we once
> believed we'd conquered, no less)?

How can we admit that our TV and other screen-time
   habits have taken us to some destructive places we're
   ashamed of?

How do we admit that these wounds from our past relationships and professional disappointments are infected
   with bitterness?

How do we acknowledge that even the work we do that
   we *say* is fueled by passion is fueled also by our fears and
   insecurities?

And when we're weary and beyond the end of ourselves,
   then what? Who pulls us away from the precipice of
   burnout when we're the ones in charge and it feels as
   though everyone is looking to us at work and at home?

It's easier to think we're supposed to do better than this, be better
than this.

*Haven't You already done enough for me as it is, Jesus? I should be
better at this by now, so don't come closer. Let me do this; let me fix this.*

*Stay away from my dirt, my sweat, my dust, my filth, my wounds,
my weakness. Stay away—You're not welcome here. I can't cope with
You here when I'm like this. Not when this is me.*

*Come and find me fresh after a pedicure, when I'm wearing my
best shoes. That's what You want to see. You'll be proud of me that way.*

That's what I want You to see.

Yet to share life with Jesus, to live with faith-shaped purpose, is
to share all that we are, to invite Him into even the most complex,
challenging, painful realities in our lives. He's already there—just let
Him in.

It's awkward and maybe a little bit scary. It's uncomfortable to sit in the reality of who we are. There's a powerlessness in acknowledging the depths of our wounds, weariness, and weaknesses. There's a help-lessness in admitting we won't bounce back from this as quickly as we'd hoped. It's certainly vulnerable, especially if we've prided our-selves on being the kinds of leaders who keep it all together. We cannot present or perform our way out of our own brokenness, no matter how hard we try.

WE CANNOT *present* OR PERFORM OUR
WAY OUT OF OUR OWN BROKENNESS,
NO MATTER HOW *hard* WE TRY.

Nevertheless, Jesus doesn't need us to keep it all together, to pre-tend life and people haven't happened to us. He's the kind of leader who tends to His leaders, lays down His life *for their whole lives.*

On that night, Jesus illustrated His concern and love for His lead-ers. With the Cross only hours away from Him, He extended an invi-tation to them—to cleanse and heal them, to renew them and serve them.

Jesus offers us the same invitation today, and it's an ongoing invi-tation for every phase of our lives—a cleansing that will wash and re-lieve our stinging wounds. It's vulnerable and we might feel completely exposed, but ultimately it delivers us to walk—even run!—into our purpose without a limp in sight, whole, cleansed, and free.

It's exciting to discover we're designed with purpose in mind: to uncover gifts and dream big, world-changing dreams. But it would be naive to pretend that living into our God-given dreams is pain-free or easy. It's not a casual stroll but rather a marathon on tough terrain. Our feet aren't always ready for what we'll find on the journey, and there are things about it we simply cannot prepare for, even if we wanted to.

An afternoon in urgent care and a follow-up appointment in the doctor's office were just two of the many triggers for "come to Jesus" moments I've experienced. They were moments when I realized that what I needed most of all was to let Jesus come to me—or even simply rediscover He was already there.

I've needed healing from the crushing words spoken about me—words that wounded so deeply they threatened my leadership journey. Or the way experiences of racism and sexism dehumanize and scar body and soul. Never mind walking with a limp—there were days I could barely crawl. There were other days when the pressure of leading was too much and, exhausted by the politics and the pressure, I wanted out.

Living into our purpose comes with all kinds of ups and downs. Good days, great days, sad days, and bad days. Days that couldn't get any better, and those that couldn't get worse.

On every single one of those days, I've needed the One who would see me as I am and wash away the weariness and be a balm to my wounds. I've needed the One who would meet me at my points of weakness and challenge me, protect me, transform me.

I've needed to create peace and take time to let Him meet with me. *Then* I can rise and walk another day.

REVIEW AND REFLECT

What areas do you prefer to keep hidden and separate, even from Jesus?

In what parts of your life do you need Jesus to "wash your feet"?

Say Yes to Who You Are

(And Why We Don't Leave Good Gifts Unwrapped)

> When I stand before God at the end of my life, I would hope that I would not have a single bit of talent left and could say, "I used everything you gave me."
>
> —ERMA BOMBECK

*C*hristmas is a huge event in the Saxton household. My youngest has a December birthday, and back when she was a preschooler, she used to declare, "I love this month. It's all about me and Jesus!" After hearing that, I knew the Christmas season wasn't likely to be a quiet affair. As far as she's concerned, the decorations, the traditions, and the food are all integral parts of celebrating—with great fanfare— the wonder that she is.

In addition, we have an extended family that stretches across four continents at any given time. So rather than a day, Christmas actually lasts for about three weeks.

Unlike the vast majority of our Minnesotan neighbors, Christmas Eve is not the big event (save for a late-night Skype call to Hong Kong for the kids to chat with their uncle and aunt). Christmas Day is *the day* when all much-requested gifts are finally unwrapped. When I was a child, we unwrapped our gifts on Christmas morning, the earlier the better.

My husband and his family did things a little differently. Every year on Christmas Day at 3:00 p.m., Queen Elizabeth addresses the Commonwealth with a Christmas message. The tradition began with her grandfather King George V in the 1930s, by radio broadcast on the BBC's Empire Service. In later years with later monarchs, the broadcast moved to black-and-white television, then color, and now 3-D. The message chronicles significant events in the year and, in Queen Elizabeth's case in recent years, it includes a spiritual reflection. It's a short message, but in my husband's family it played a central role in the Christmas festivities. Much to my husband's childhood frustration, Christmas gifts were not to be opened until *after* the Queen's speech. At 3:00 p.m.! Can you imagine trying to keep children away from their longed-for gifts until three in the afternoon?

Though my British Nigerian immigrant family had an unexpected affection for the Queen and the royals (and never missed watching a televised royal wedding), we did not build our day around the Queen's speech. By 3:00 p.m., we were eating (or preparing to eat again), talking with relatives who dropped by, or opening more presents. If there wasn't music playing, then *perhaps* the Queen's Christmas message was on the TV in the background, a faint backdrop to our lives. So when my husband and I got together and we talked about family traditions we'd like to continue, he was determined that this would *not* be one of them (though I do admit I quite like to watch it online).

Our kids are ready for the Christmas Day celebrations at dawn. One year, my firstborn was ready while it was still dark. She came into our room at 3:00 a.m., wished us a merry Christmas, and then, overwhelmed by excitement, promptly vomited in three parts of the house, none of which were in a sink or a toilet.

Years later they still don't play it cool. You see, they've been preparing. In recent years, they have upgraded their gift requests from incessant begging to a slick, cool PowerPoint presentation. Something for us to pore over and then "please send around the world" to family members. My youngest tends to have a list of anything and everything she could possibly think of (she likes to give options). My eldest is more strategic in her approach: the gift at the top of the list is not the one she really wants. That gift is somewhere between numbers three and five and is usually expensive. She hopes it slips in without anyone noticing. *We see you, kiddo!*

When the strategies and slideshows and plea bargaining are done and Christmas morning arrives, that's when the fun truly begins. Gifts are handed out and nearly torn to pieces, and the living room is transformed into a sea of wrapping paper and string and bows. There are always treasures to be found: practical necessities (socks!), new board games, and so on.

As they've gotten older, they've also found a deep love for gift cards since they can spend them freely in their favorite stores. Then after the squeals, the thank-yous, and the hugs, they disappear for what seems like hours. The kids can be found around the house, deep in their latest book, reading the rules for the game they received, try-ing on new clothes, messing around with their most recent gadget, and contacting friends to compare notes.

As much as I moan about it, I love it. I love seeing the joy on their faces. I love giving them the things they need and some of the things they want. I love seeing the thoughtfulness that has gone into the gifts they buy each other and things they choose or create for their father and me. I love it because I love my kids and want to see them thrive in every possible way.

I'm not unique in that; I'm just an everyday parent. I'm someone who likes to see people enjoy the gifts they've been given.

That's how it's supposed to be with gifts, isn't it? They are meant to be unwrapped, discovered, explored, and enjoyed. That new bike is supposed to be taken for a ride; that new game is supposed to be played; the socks are supposed to be worn. We'd think it was strange—more than that, we'd be saddened—if the gifts were left untouched.

Imagine a different scene on Christmas morning with my girls. The gifts are piled high around the tree, gifts with my daughters' names on them. They run toward them, they even pick them up, but they're subdued and uncertain. My eldest unwraps the gift that was number four on her list, the one she really wanted, and she squeals with joy and then, sadly, wraps it back up again and pushes it behind the tree. My youngest looks at her gifts with her name neatly printed on the tag and keeps asking, "Are they mine? Are you sure they don't belong to someone else?"

They unwrap games and gadgets but place them down, leaving them untouched, and when I ask them why, they respond,

"Suppose I play it wrong? Suppose I break it or something?"

"Do you want to return it to the store?"

"No, I love it—really I do. I just don't want to mess it up, that's all."

Finally they are persuaded to take the socks, the notebooks for school, and all the practical everyday things under the tree. Even then, they're not relaxed, but at least they take them.

And the other gifts? They leave them under the tree. Long after the lights blink out, the presents are still there, gathering dust, now just part of the living room furniture. The game that is supposed to be played with friends they invite to sleepovers, the bike that is supposed to be ridden around the neighborhood or to school as they begin to sprout their fledgling wings of independence, the book series that they would normally immerse themselves in.

It's a cluttered room, but we won't clear it away—not even the cute stuff we added in the stockings and Christmas bags, even though the girls didn't ask for them—because every single thing in this room is theirs. We're just waiting for our girls to recognize it. Sometimes the gift one of them needs is right there under the tree, but for some reason she won't take it. Most of the time, the kids' lives are so busy they simply run through the room without paying attention to the gifts that wait to be picked up and enjoyed.

It's a depressing illustration, and it seems highly improbable, doesn't it? What children are going to ignore or abandon the gifts that their loving parents have given them—gifts they want and might have even asked for?

Yet although it sounds utterly unrealistic, it turns out this happens all the time.

Many of us live this way on a daily basis. Especially women.

God is the gift giver. God is *our* gift giver. And all too often we are like hesitant, nervous children, questioning the gifts under the tree. We leave them lying idle, gathering dust.

Our Creator, our heavenly Father, the ultimate parent, has lavished on us a generous, wide range of incredible gifts, talents, skills, and abilities.

> GOD IS THE GIFT GIVER. GOD IS *OUR*
> GIFT GIVER. AND ALL TOO OFTEN WE ARE
> LIKE HESITANT, nervous CHILDREN,
> QUESTIONING THE GIFTS UNDER THE
> TREE. WE LEAVE THEM LYING idle,
> GATHERING DUST.

There are abilities we have developed that we weren't always great at initially. If it was riding a bike, we always fell off! But over time, with some practice and perseverance, we got better, until it came so naturally to us that we forgot we ever had to learn.

Then there are the gifts that we have no explanation for. They are part of us, and when we unwrap those, it seems a bit like a whisper from heaven because there's something a little bit special, God given, about them. Somehow when they operate in our lives, they seem to have God's smile on them. Something about those are naturally supernatural.

You'd think with gifts like these, we'd celebrate from the rooftops. Huge gifts from a good Father, a Father who delighted to give us these gifts, who lavishes gifts on us because He loves us and because those gifts can be life giving to us and those around us. You'd think we wouldn't be able to stop celebrating.

Sadly, that's not always the case.

> We're afraid of that gift, we don't understand how it works,
> and we've forgotten that it's okay to learn—that that's
> actually part of the fun—so we quietly put it back under
> the tree.
> We tried that gift, but other people were critical of it.
> It wasn't a popular gift or the right gift for someone like
> us. We felt embarrassed. Other people felt uncomfortable
> with our gift, which in turn made us uncomfortable.
> The gift became cumbersome, burdensome. It upset the
> balance of our friendships and other relationships.

So . . . we put it back in its box, resealed the wrapping paper, and put it back under the tree.

We didn't use it anymore. We played down and denied its existence, and we called our denial humility.

We didn't talk about it anymore to God or to anyone. There were some gifts we just avoided, thinking, *I know that's a gift with my name on it, and I'm intrigued, but isn't that gift only for men? Why has it been given to me? I don't remember including that in my Power-Point presentation!* We scribble out our names and leave the gift there, hoping someone else will lay claim to it.

Some of the gifts seem so ordinary we dismiss them. Is there even a gift of cooking, for crying out loud? Or making a bed for someone who needs it at short notice? It's *just* managing a home. It's *just* running a budget—it's what we went to college to learn. It's only organization—it's a practical way to live. There are no dreams or grand visions around it—they are just basic necessities that help us function. Isn't it a bit of an embellishment to wrap it up in fancy language and stick a pretentious bow on it and make it sound more meaningful than it is? It's not special, just normal. Surely anyone can do it. And although this gift is not left under the tree, its value and potential in the lives of others are discarded like old wrapping paper.

Over the years, I've noticed the way women sometimes downplay their influence and impact with the use of the word *just* or *only*. *"I'm just a mom." "I'm only an assistant." "I'm just a grandmother." "I'm only a college student." Just* and *only* can sometimes make us believe our contributions are insignificant or inadequate. It's not true. So while the ordinary basic-necessity skills we possess aren't a big deal to us, they're actually so valuable that they could be used to help someone else, love someone else, transform someone else—for life. Furthermore, we can sometimes conclude that our roles disqualify us from wider leadership and influence. As former White House secretary Dee Dee Myers once reflected, "I am endlessly fascinated that playing football is considered a training ground for leadership, but raising children isn't."[1]

There are the gifts that are like seeds waiting to be sown, ideas and dreams embedded in our hearts and minds that will take time to unfold and need our attention. But the fact that we don't know all the details and how it will all work out can be intimidating. They feel too scary to feel like gifts, so we don't just leave them under the tree; we kick them behind the couch next to the tree and try to forget they are there.

We've forgotten something important: they were always gifts from a good Father (see James 1:17), a Father who knew exactly what we needed and even saw things we wanted but couldn't articulate. A good Father who knew that as we learned how to use some of these gifts, they would become life-giving sources to us and life-giving resources to other people. He knew what gifts would take practice and perseverance, but ultimately they were gifts He delighted to give.

What if we had misunderstood our gifts and talents? It seems we've extended our grading systems beyond the academic world and used them in the areas of our worth and gifting. Consequently, it's not enough to enjoy a gift and celebrate the way we've been wired. Our gift has to be the best—the most popular, most recognized, and maybe a little monetized.

Think about this: Our understanding of the value of our gifts— and, by extension, *our* value—is blurred and confused by the way skills are monetized in our world and by the accepted views on what we "ought to" or "should" be doing or accomplishing. We've idolized certain skills and abilities, treating some as more glamorous and special; we've viewed some as more valuable. Who wouldn't want those gifts?

Yet in a podcast discussion on gender inequality with Malcolm Gladwell, former Australian prime minister Julia Gillard contended that we need "a profound reworking of what we think merit is."[2] She contended that studies show that even our understanding of merit is based on gender. A man and a woman possessing the same gifts and qualities were not deemed equally valuable or employable. They couldn't unwrap the same gifts under the tree and be treated the same way. The woman was more likely to be viewed suspiciously for "acting like a man" and passed over for a position.

Perhaps that woman should leave that gift behind and find ones that other people consider more acceptable.

Another distortion of the way we understand our gifts and skills is that, too often, acknowledging our gifts is perceived as arrogant, prideful, and selfishly ambitious (we'll come back to ambition later) instead of being seen as simply receiving what our loving God has delighted to give. Perhaps acknowledging and enjoying the gifts you've been given can have far more to do with your relationship with God the gift giver and far less to do with what people around you (who may or may not be watching) think about you using them.

If unwrapping your gifts was exactly what the Father wanted from you, using them fully is simply the overflow of a heavenly Father's loving relationship with His child. God is simply inviting you to partner with Him in the renewal of a broken world around you.

Would you unwrap your gifts then?

No permission slip is needed; we mustn't wait for a speech late in the day as a cue to move forward. Simply unwrap the gifts and skills and talents He has given you, and use them in every way possible in your everyday life.

It may sound strange to view using our gifts and talents so positively and freely, because our cultural conditioning has made us afraid or insecure about our gifts. We're not expected to admit being gifted or skilled or talented in any way, let alone enjoy it. Somehow we've even made it superspiritual and borderline "pseudo holy" to *not* mention them!

There's nothing wrong with embracing the way God has wired you, gifted you, and created you. It *is* wonderful, because you *are* wonderfully made. Read Psalm 139 for confirmation. There is nothing wrong with saying yes to who you are in God! There is nothing wrong with saying yes to the gifts and skills and talents God delighted to give you!

In fact, it's essential if we are to understand what it means to live with Him and for Him. It's integral to understanding what it means to live as image bearers.

IMAGE. LIKENESS. REIGN.

When God created human beings, He spoke of their purpose:

> God said, "Let us make human beings in our image, to be like us. They will reign over the fish in the sea, the birds in the sky, the livestock, all the wild animals on the earth, and the small animals that scurry along the ground."
>
> So God created human beings in his own image.
> In the image of God he created them;
> male and female he created them.
>
> Then God blessed them and said, "Be fruitful and multiply. Fill the earth and govern it. Reign over the fish in the sea, the birds in the sky, and all the animals that scurry along the ground."

Then God said, "Look! I have given you every seed-
bearing plant throughout the earth and all the fruit trees for
your food. And I have given every green plant as food for all
the wild animals, the birds in the sky, and the small animals
that scurry along the ground—everything that has life." And
that is what happened.

Then God looked over all he had made, and he saw that
it was very good! (Genesis 1:26–31, NLT)

In the Creation account, the Spirit of God moves across the void
and creates out of the chaos, speaking the world into existence, calling
it all good. Light. Day and night. Sky. Land and water. Vegetation.
Sun. Moon. Stars and constellations. Living creatures. All of creation,
bursting and blooming with life and beauty and vitality. God is speaking, moving, working—and it's incredible!

The Creation journey reaches its zenith when God creates human
beings. It's not that the previous acts of Creation are somehow insignificant, but God's description of humanity and words to them are
important:

"Let us make mankind in our *image,* in our *likeness*" (Genesis
1:26, emphasis added).

Or

"Let us make human beings in our *image,* to be *like us*" (NLT,
emphasis added).

The word for image (*tselem*) means shape, resemblance, a shadow
or an outline of something original. In practice, it means a "representative figure."[3] The word *likeness* echoes the understanding of tselem,

bringing powerful added emphasis and volume (surround sound!) to what God has to say.

Humanity is made with the imprint, the deep impression of God on their very nature. The "image" is no illusion; it is the reality. God created human beings with qualities and abilities and faculties that resemble and reflect something of His own nature. The added understanding of tselem reveals even more of the scope of the *imago Dei*.

As representative figures of God, human beings have a practical role to play on the earth. They not only resemble Him but they are also commissioned to represent Him in the land they have been given. It's a bold calling. In the ancient world, this was a radical view because "only kings and queens were considered representatives of deity."[4] Wealth, power, and privilege were the pathways to value and worth.

The Creation narratives tear that worldview to shreds because Elohim (God) speaks a different word. Value, worth, and agency are actually given by the Creator. All human beings simply carry the family traits—the family likeness. This is not just for the special ones, the wealthy and talented, the royal; this is for each and every one of us.

Thus, men and women are both, together, commissioned to "reign" over this newly created vast expanse of a beautiful earth—to steward it in ways that represent our Creator (see Psalm 8:6–9). We're invited to close relationship with Him; we continue that family likeness, generation after generation. What worlds will our words create? Where will we bring light in the darkness? Order in the midst of turbulent, powerful chaos? Vibrant beauty and creativity? What brings new life that resources others? Will our lives brim and burst with God's care and vitality and glory and power as we represent Him? Will people glimpse something of the heart and mind and nature of our God through who we are and what we do with all we have been given?

To be absolutely clear, we are not gods; God is God. Yet we have the imprint of God on our lives, the impression of the Creator deeply imbedded in us, making us image bearers, created ones, with gifts and talents and abilities that were not a concession but a delight as God created us.

That way you have with numbers, that artistic ability, that passion, that strategic mind, your skills with data analysis, your hospitality gift, that compassionate heart, those leadership qualities, those things you just do because they are a part of you—they didn't start with you. They began with a God who considers you fearfully and wonderfully made, and His works are wonderful.

Your gifts and abilities are not accidents; they are gifts from your Creator, who already saw you as valuable and worthy. *Loved.* Those gifts and qualities intrinsic to the very nature of God are reminders of the family likeness. They are part of His plan for you to represent Him in the world.

Surely it's time to say yes to who you are and how your Creator has wired you. Surely it's time to embrace the family likeness He's given and know you are worthy and loved. Surely it's time to identify the gifts under the tree and the ones you have tucked behind the tree and dust them off and use them. No more hiding your gifting and calling it humility; no more being trapped by fear and shame. Unwrap the gifts your Creator has given you. Enjoy them and use them to represent Him in and through your life. Use them in service to a cause bigger than yourself.

Your world is waiting.

A Conversation, in Theory

For our second gathering, everyone arrived at the meal on time.

"Can we unpack the question as we eat?" asked Bree, to murmurs of agreement around the table.

"Sure!" I replied, pleased that everyone was ready and willing to dive straight in.

"It'll give us more time," Bree continued. "And if it gets really heavy, we can always order dessert."

I smiled. "Okay, let's do it. I'll set the scene for you. It's Christmastime, and your heavenly Father has placed many packages for you under the Christmas tree. The packages represent your talents, skills, and personality traits. However, a number of the packages are gathering dust because you've refused to unwrap them for years. Others are unwrapped but hidden away in and around the tree, and the Father wants you to unwrap them too." I paused. "What gifts [skills, talents, and so on] have you hidden or left unwrapped for a long time and why?"

The women were silent for a painfully awkward length of time. I began to wonder if I'd pushed them a little too hard and expected a little too much from a group of women who'd met not long ago.

Rachel turned to me slowly and inquired, "Do you ever ask lighthearted questions?"

The table erupted in laughter, breaking the tension. Bree called out to one of the passing restaurant staff. "Excuse me, miss? We're going to need the dessert menu over here, please. One for each of us!"

Okay. It was the right question. "Would you like to go first, Rachel?"

"Not before the tiramisu gets here."

"I'll go," volunteered Angela. "This question is a good one for me. Well, as some of you know, I've worked in corporate all my career. That's the place of influence for me. I have to admit, I'd not thought of my skill set as a gift from God or as part of that image-bearing thing. Throughout my life, I have felt that my skill set has been a problem, a bit too much. I was a tomboy, but it was more than that. I was seen as tough, strong, too bossy or directive. My mom used to despair of me, worrying about how a girl like me would ever settle down."

She sighed. "Anyway, I've often felt the church doesn't know what to do with me. I don't fit into the mold of a 'church woman.' I don't go to the Bible studies because I am often in a team meeting or on a work trip. On my worst and maybe even my most cynical days, I begin to think they [the church leaders] only like me and want me included because of my money. Maybe that's harsh, but I'm not going to sugarcoat my feelings, because do they value my skills as a contribution? Maybe they don't know what to do with a woman like me, working in a fast-paced career, making the corporate climb.

"But, honestly, I could really use the support. Success has come at a heavy price sometimes. I've never understood why the church spends so little time investing in the place where its congregation spends the vast majority of its waking hours."

I leaned forward and looked directly at Angela. "Thanks for sharing that, Angela. I think your story raises a number of important points. I'm sorry your church experience has been alienating. Before I go on, though, does anyone here identify specifically with Angela's story?"

"Where you said 'They don't know what to do with a woman like me,'" said CeCe.

I saw a flicker of relief in Angela's face as she asked, "You've been through something similar?"

"For me, it's the feeling that I'm too strong, that I'm too vocal or direct when I give a report to the board meeting for our nonprofit."

Angela nodded. "Oh yes, too direct. I wonder if they want me to lie or make it up."

"Right?" said CeCe animatedly. I could tell these two women were going to become good friends, so I sat back to enjoy watching it happen.

CeCe continued, "Sometimes the truth is direct. But I get the feeling there is a cultural thing, an expectation there. They like me, yet I'm told that to fit in with the organization, I need to be quieter, less confrontational—that It's how change will come. I'm all for healthy compromise and good communication, don't get me wrong. But it's like I have to speak a different way, to the point where I'm a different woman. I feel I can't be myself there. I have to put part of me away to get anything done. So, to your question." CeCe turned to me. "The idea of God wanting me to unwrap my gifts is challenging. I don't think people want me to be myself. They want me to acquiesce."

"I hear you, CeCe," I replied. "That's tough." Then I paused. I knew there weren't easy, neat responses to either Angela's or CeCe's experiences, but we each needed to hear them, to feel them, for a moment. I wanted these women to feel seen and heard. One idea popped into my mind, though, so after a few more seconds, I took a deep breath and then said, "You know, it's a shame these spaces don't appear to recognize the *ezer* thing. Then they'd actually understand the package you came in!"

Angela looked puzzled. "What ezer thing?"

"I was hoping you'd say that." I smiled and continued, "It's in Genesis 2. It's the first word in the Bible to describe a woman. It's translated *helper.* It's not that the word *helper* is inaccurate; it's that our understanding of the word is incomplete. Ezer is a combination of two Hebrew words meaning 'to rescue and save and be strong.'"

"Strong?" Angela asked.

"Oh, there's more. As a verb it means 'to protect, surround, defend, cherish.'[5] Most of the time when the word appears in the text, it's God rescuing His people from their enemies. The helper was one who had the power and resources to help. And the word often appears with military connotations. The ezer is a warrior."

"I loved learning about this word in seminary," said Kate. "It was a game changer!"

"It's important for each of us to know," I continued. "Some of the unhelpful stereotypes about women are when we're described or depicted in weak and fragile terms. We're depicted as helpless and overly emotional. A woman's vulnerability and tears are seen as evidence of weakness. And the limited idea of the helper has often been used to reinforce that and justify decisions, even beyond the walls of the church.

"Yet looking at the text, I think understanding ezer builds a bigger picture. I just think these parts of you that you feel aren't often received well in the church are really just an expression of what being an ezer looks like in practice. Like we all are. We women aren't all the same. Just look around this table! Where on earth did we get the idea that womanhood—biblical woman-hood, if you will—expresses itself in only one particular way? We don't see it in the women in the Bible, and we don't see it today. The idea of an ezer articulates something about our God-given DNA."

Most of the women were looking at one another and smiling at this point. I was glad they were encouraged, but I noticed that Bree looked uncomfortable. I hoped she felt able to push back if needed, safe enough to say what was on her mind.

"Angela and CeCe," began Bree, "let me begin by saying I'm frustrated by your experiences, and I'm so sorry they happened to you. You've got me thinking about some of the women in our community who I've simply overlooked and assumed were disin-terested. But . . ." Bree's voice drifted off as her nerves increased.

"But there's something you want to say, right?" I prodded.

"I don't know what your church backgrounds are, but my environment might be a bit more conservative than yours, or maybe it's that *I* am. I've always believed that my role *was* sup-portive, and I'm happy with that. I don't feel oppressed or held back. I believe a supportive role is my calling. I think it's just how I'm wired."

"I appreciate your bringing that up, Bree. It's always a risk to say where you stand among new friends. I convened this group because I believe women can lead freely, wherever they feel called. I think it's helpful to see what being an ezer means for us as image-bearing women rather than live believing something is fundamentally wrong with us for the way God wired us. So I want to affirm and celebrate your calling too. Unwrap your gifts, Bree!"

I continued, "I expected we'd have different views at this table on what our leadership might look like in practice. We may interpret the implications of the word *ezer* and its application differently. That's okay; we're here to listen and learn from one another." Looking around the table, I said, "I hope we all feel safe to share freely."

At the end of the evening, Angela approached me. Though she stood immaculate and poised, for a moment she also looked vulnerable, weary. "*Ezer*. No one has ever said that to me before. I was always too much, too strong, too ambitious. But I see I'm ezer too. No one has ever told me that." She paused, nodding and fighting to maintain her composure. Finally she took in a deep breath. "Thank you," she said. Then she smiled and left.

> **ezer:** "to rescue, to save, to be strong," often translated *helper* in Genesis 2:18. Facts about the word *ezer:*
> - There are more than a hundred references to its root in the Old Testament.
> - Twenty-one references use the identical word.
> - Two times describe the woman.

- Three times refer to military aid.
- Sixteen times mention God as the helper of His people, using powerful military language.
- *Ezer* often appears in parallel with words denoting strength and power.
- It means "the helper"—one who had the power to help.
- It can be used as a noun or a verb, meaning to defend, protect, surround, and cherish.[6]

REVIEW AND REFLECT

It's Christmastime, and your heavenly Father placed many packages for you under the Christmas tree. The packages represent your talents, skills, and personality traits. However, a number of the packages are gathering dust because you've refused to unwrap them for years. Others were partially unwrapped, then put back under the tree. Still, the Father wants you to recognize and enjoy every gift that He's given you.

What gifts (skills, talents, personality traits) have you hidden or left unwrapped for a long time and why?

A Voice Without Apology

(And What "Too Much" Really Means)

> Women don't need to find a voice, they have a voice,
> and they need to feel empowered to use it, and people
> need to be encouraged to listen.
>
> —MEGHAN MARKLE, Duchess of Sussex

The atmosphere was thrilling. Deborah could see her people, thousands of them, moving toward her and the army. Some were running, some were dancing, some hobbled, and others were carried, but all were moving. They'd come from the villages and the towns across the region. She could hear voices shouting, laughing, screaming, and even some wailing. It was the laughter that moved her the most. It had been such a long time since she'd seen many of her people smile or laugh.

Music filled the air. Drums beating, people clapping their hands and stomping their feet, all in rhythm. She looked down and realized she was stomping too, in rhythm. Instead of the sound of marching that had terrorized her people for years, these were the celebratory footsteps of the free.

Deborah turned toward the people by her side. Looking over her shoulder, she saw her husband, Lappidoth. He was staring directly at her. He nodded slowly and smiled at her, the way he did for only her. Always for her. She held his gaze for an extra moment and returned his smile.

Barak stood next to her, looking at the crowd. He stood up straighter than she'd ever seen him stand. This was who she always knew he could be. It was satisfying to see him that way. Next to him were other warriors, tribal leaders who had been reluctant to go to war. They'd held back and tried to hold Barak back, but now they claimed the victory as theirs too. A flame of frustration burned in her heart, but she suppressed it. There would be time for conversations, she resolved.

As her eyes scanned other faces, she saw *her* standing there. Jael. She walked over to her and took both of Jael's hands in her own. They smiled and laughed, tears streaming down their cheeks, the same fire in their eyes. The world would know that this woman, Jael, was the hero of their story. Deborah would make sure of it.

It was time. She returned to her place in front of this joyous people, these free people.

Deborah raised her hands, her arms outstretched as if to encompass an entire nation. The people cheered for Deborah; they screamed, shouted, and sang praises to God. She smiled and laughed with her arms open wide, encouraging their voices to rise—louder, louder. She wanted them to hear their own voices, their own joy, their own grief, their own praise. It had always been there—it just had been denied for so long.

Finally, Deborah took a deep breath and began to sing,

When the princes in Israel take the lead,
    When the people willingly offer themselves—
    Praise the LORD! (Judges 5:2)

———

For twenty years, the Israelites had been oppressed by Jabin, king of Canaan. Sisera, Jabin's army commander, led a military unit with weaponry more sophisticated and powerful than anything the Israelites could hope to use. Inevitably, the people succumbed to the intimidating daily brutality of military rule. The roads were unsafe, and travelers had to find alternate routes for fear of being robbed. The villages were also dangerous, and people fled their communities to walled towns for their own protection (see Judges 5:6–7). Eventually occupation and oppression became normalized. Elders passed from this life to the next without promise of hope or assurance of the generation they left behind. Children grew into adults with no other framework for their lives. Even though this was a painful new reality for some, for the young, emerging generation of Israelites, it was all they had ever known. After twenty years, God's people *finally* voiced their desperation and cried out to God for help. Enter Deborah.

THIS. GIRL. IS. ON. FIRE.

Deborah was a powerful, wise, and strong leader. A judge and a prophetess, she was her community's spiritual and civil leader. She led, secure in her authority and role, even in challenging circumstances.

Her leadership shatters the common stereotypes of women in leadership and breaks through the expectations to show what we can be. The text notes that Deborah is a married woman, wife of Lappidoth (Judges 4:4). But the phrase *wife of Lappidoth* has more than one meaning. It also means "woman of torches" or "fiery woman."[1] I think the words speak of both Deborah's marital status and her character as a woman on fire with a God-fueled, passionate, and strong voice in her nation. Maybe like the fellow prophet Jeremiah, she, too, lived with fire in her bones, with God's unstoppable words in her heart (see Jeremiah 20:9).

AFTER ALL, OUR *Voices* ARE MORE
THAN MERE WORDS. OUR VOICES
ARE OUR GOD-GIVEN IDENTITY AND
purpose IN ACTION.

Yet the full power of Deborah's voice was not limited to the words she spoke or the song she would sing. After all, our voices are more than mere words. Our voices are our God-given identity and purpose in action. In her book *Raise Your Voice,* writer and speaker Kathy Khang reminds us that "our voice—our influence and our interaction with people and the world around us—is embodied through our words *and* actions."[2] Deborah used her voice in its fullest capacity and models for us ways we can use our own.

In the Trenches of Our Everyday Relationships and Conflicts

Deborah governed from the Palm of Deborah in the hill country of Ephraim (see Judges 4:5). There she met with men and women on a daily basis, handling disputes too complicated for local judges, dealing with people's everyday drama and trauma.[3] She processed and spoke into the burdens of the nation. Sometimes using your voice isn't about the public spaces and crowds; it's more personal, gritty, and everyday.

Hearing and Voicing God's Heart for His People

As the spiritual leader of the community, Deborah listened to God when He seemed to be far from His people. It is no surprise the nation relied on her leadership. In turbulent and terrifying times, Deborah was the influential voice of guidance, leadership, and spiritual insight. She was also the catalyst for change, transformation, and deliverance of God's people for a generation. Sometimes using your voice means representing God's heart and values to those around you, speaking and living prophetically amid cultural upheaval.

Courageous Conversations

As Israel's judge, Deborah also oversaw the military. She summoned Barak to be her general and gave him God-given instructions to gather an army of ten thousand men to fight Sisera and his military might, promising God would "give him into [Barak's] hands" (Judges 4:7). Some translations read these instructions differently, and instead of

Deborah starting her conversation with Barak by saying, "The LORD, the God of Israel, commands you" (verse 6), she began, "Didn't the Lord, the God of Israel, command you?" suggesting Barak might have had these instructions for some time and was holding back. Deborah wasn't afraid to use her voice to confront and challenge when required.

Barak's response was conditional. He would go to war against Sisera only if Deborah went with him. It's no surprise Barak wasn't confident, even if he had heard God. He'd lived through twenty years of intimidation and oppression, seeing Sisera's sophisticated weaponry crush his people. Perhaps it also crushed his confidence in God or his confidence in hearing from God or his confidence to lead. After losing their villages and highways to Sisera and his men for twenty years, how could they possibly expect to win now?

Barak had lost his voice under the crushing weight of oppression. He *needed* Deborah's influence, her spiritual leadership—her *voice*—in order to risk the wrath of Sisera and indeed risk his own life. He needed to know that God was on his side and Deborah was His representative. Perhaps Barak felt that the ten thousand men he'd call to risk their lives and join him needed the same. Deborah agreed but told Barak his reluctance to believe God's words *to him* would cost him the ultimate prize in battle: Sisera. Now Sisera would be taken out by a woman.

Sometimes our voices are needed for courageous conversations. Sometimes our voices give other people the courage to find theirs.

A VOICE THAT LEADS UNAPOLOGETICALLY

It was Deborah who described God's military strategy for the battle (see Judges 4:6–7). And it was Deborah who gave the war cry to the gathered tribes of Israel. Deborah's voice empowered people to fight for freedom and receive their deliverance. Her voice sang their story when the battle was won.

Deborah didn't dial herself down in the presence of others. She didn't edit the acknowledgment of her contribution in a quest for (false) humility. She was bold, and in her victory song before an entire nation, she owned and named her place in the story. She didn't hide who she was or what she brought to the table. No, she owned it and talked—sang!—about who she was and what she had done.

> In the days of Shamgar son of Anath,
> in the days of Jael, the highways were abandoned;
> travelers took to winding paths.
> Villagers in Israel would not fight;
> they held back until I, Deborah, arose,
> until I arose, a mother in Israel. (5:6–7)

Mother in Israel? Some scholars note that the reference as mother could refer to Deborah's biological motherhood, showing that a mother's role can extend as far as the corridors of political power.[4] More often, scholars understand *mother* as a title of honor for an authority figure, a protector in the community.[5] "As a mother, Deborah provided military and political security for all of her children," wrote professor and priest Wilda C. Gafney.[6] In addition, theologian and author Dr. Linda Belleville states that "in Israel" is recognition of Deborah's national leadership role.[7] Deborah was secure enough to voice and articulate the broad scope of her leadership and influence in her society.

There are times when the hardest voice to elevate is your own—

especially if you are a woman, particularly if you're a woman on the margins. It's not always seen as culturally acceptable to tell people the full extent of who you are. For all the talk of showing up and being courageous in our culture, in some contexts it's seen as arrogant and offensive to do so. Humility is seen as quiet and deprecating, and hiding is seen as holy. Yet here Deborah is, speaking of the impact of her contribution with a before and after. Here is Deborah telling people about her position in society, the level of her authority. She doesn't appear to be squirming either.

There are times when using your voice means articulating who you are—the skills you bring and the impact you make. It certainly means advocating on behalf of others, but it also can mean amplifying and advocating for yourself. Could you? Would you?

A Raised Voice Raises Up Other Voices

Deborah's influence created an environment where, in the face of oppression and fear, God's people could rise up and challenge the status quo. Her courage inspired and ignited courage in her people—not only in the once-intimidated Barak or the armies of God's people but also in an unexpected heroine called Jael. When Sisera realizes he's about to be defeated, he runs away until he arrives at Jael's tent, expecting protection and a chance for rest. Jael welcomes him, and while he sleeps, she kills him, thus ending twenty years of terror for the Israelites.

When we use our voices, our influence, when we show up in our own lives and callings, others are strengthened, invited, and empowered to do the same.

HOLD ON—IS THIS WOMAN'S VOICE TOO MUCH?

Some theologians aren't kind to Deborah or Jael. They describe these women's leadership as unfeminine, too masculine and aggressive, and express some disappointment in their accomplishments or minimize their influence. One leader even suggests that although Deborah was successful in her career, she was not successful as a homemaker.[8] Another wishes Deborah had used her influence "in the quieter ways of life."[9] Jael's conquering of Sisera is considered "more like the work of a fiend than a woman."[10]

WHEN WE USE OUR VOICES, OUR INFLUENCE, WHEN WE *show up* IN OUR OWN LIVES AND CALLINGS, OTHERS ARE STRENGTHENED, INVITED, AND *empowered* TO DO THE SAME.

It's worth noting these actions aren't happening during peacetime. These are challenging choices made during an attempt to overthrow evil after decades of oppression. There have been warrior women throughout history who have fought for their people, from Boudica to Amina of Zazzau, from the sainted Joan of Arc to women faithfully serving in the military today. Deborah and Jael and women like them are serving their nations in wartime.

Perhaps a broader picture of womanhood and femininity is needed—and deserved.

Deborah mentions another set of women in her victory song:

Sisera's mom and her attendants. As Sisera's mother wonders when her
son is due to return home, her attendants note that it's likely he and his
army are looking at the plunder and choosing "a woman or two for
each man" (Judges 5:30). The attendants saw this act of taking women
of a conquered community against their will for the men's own sexual
pleasure as an inevitable part—a reward, even—of winning a war.
Deborah and Jael understood that if Sisera won, he and his army
would not only steal their possessions but also systematically commit
sexual atrocities upon the women in their community. This moment
didn't need these ezers to live so-called quieter ways of life, nor did it
need Deborah or Jael to have the perfect home. This moment required
the ezers to be warriors and fight for their people's freedom and particularly for the women in their community. This moment needed
their fully embodied voices amid the devastating brutality of war.

Deborah's influence made it possible for Jael to end Sisera's life
and deliver a nation. Deborah hails Jael as "most blessed of women"
(verse 24). It's interesting that the only other person who receives such
an accolade in the Bible is Mary, the mother of Jesus.

Have you ever felt that your voice was too much, or not good
enough? Your voice and influence might not win a popularity contest
and might be misunderstood, but does that mean you shouldn't use it?

A VOICE WITH A LEGACY

Most of all, we see Deborah's influence in her legacy. The book of
Judges is filled with warfare and violence and struggle, yet it captures
Deborah's impact with a simple sentence at the close of her story:
"Then the land had peace forty years" (5:31).

———

I've read Deborah's story many times, and I'm left wondering,

> *What if she hadn't used her voice?*
> *What if she hadn't owned her influence?*
> *What if she hadn't shared the words God had given her?*

We have the privilege of knowing how the story ended and the lasting impact of Deborah's leadership at the time. Still, it's not hard to imagine how differently the story might have ended if Deborah had hidden or held back her gifts:

> *What if she'd chosen to stay silent?*
> *What if she'd decided that it wasn't worth it, that the risk*
>   *was too great?*
> *What if she'd believed that no one would value what she*
>   *had to say?*
> *What if she'd concluded that it wasn't her job because she*
>   *was a married woman?*
> *What if she'd concluded it was too hard, too painful, and*
>   *too much and that she wasn't enough for the job?*

What if . . . ? I know the questions seem repetitive, incessant, and annoying. But it's what-if questions like these that occupy mental and emotional space in women, holding them back from using their voices every single day. It's what-if questions like these (or the fear of their answers) that have gnawed at me and left me voiceless in every stage of my life, these ordinary one-on-one conversations that I simply didn't have.

There was that time I should have asked myself where the ambiguous relationship with that cute guy was headed. We spent so much time together, connected deeply, assumed we'd be spending time together on weekends and never invited anyone else. I wanted to know what we were, where it was going—unless the answer wasn't the one I wanted. So I didn't ask and didn't share what I felt or hoped or expected from a relationship. I didn't walk away because I was muted by fear of feeling rejected and alone.

Or the many times when someone asked me how I was doing and I didn't answer truthfully that I was low, afraid, or insecure. I was afraid of the vulnerability, theirs and mine. It didn't feel like bravery to be honest about my struggles; it felt like risking exposure and hurt. What would I do if I wasn't taken seriously? So instead, I silenced myself, my heart, my traumas.

It wasn't easier to use my voice for others in the trenches either. I've had moments when I feared my words would be pointless and shallow. I felt ill equipped to talk someone else through pain bigger than my own mind could fathom, forgetting that my embodied voice could hold a hand. So instead of saying a clunky word, I held back. I held back from the conversations that required courage from me and might inspire courage or bring comfort or simply make me present to others.

My what-ifs silenced the stirrings to respond to God's voice. I worried, *What if I'm wrong?* Surely it was safer, wiser, to ignore the signs and promptings, even when it left me conflicted. When it came to my voice as influential, as engagement with the world around me, the questions just got louder and harder. Who did I think I was to even want to be influential? Did I believe my voice mattered just because I wanted it to, because I was passionate?

But self-doubt wasn't the only problem. Even when I wanted to speak, my words weren't always welcome. It wasn't polite to talk about gender, women in leadership, the role of women in society at large, or the stories of sexual harassment and assault agonizingly captured in the hashtag #MeToo.

It certainly wasn't polite to talk about race. I was advised that when I typed #BlackLivesMatter on social media, people found my hashtags off-putting, alienating. The sponsorship we sought as we planted a church wouldn't come. I needed to find more accessible, user-friendly terms to share my thoughts. Supposedly I'd expressed my experiences too passionately. Worse still, too angrily. Perhaps it would be better if I talked about things "calmly," "reasonably," "logically." Now I was being militant and divisive.

What happens when your voice sounds like a scream that doesn't stop? Is it worth hearing then? Maybe silence is comfortable for your listeners, but it wasn't comfortable for me.

It's a stark contrast to Deborah's unapologetic approach. Her unapologetic voice. The way she openly recognized and publicly owned her impact, credentials, and influence. And then she articulated it in word *and* song! It's natural to assume that you find your voice in the area of your qualities and accomplishments when you finally are at the top of your game—when you've actually got something to sing about, as it were. But it's not automatically the case.

Janice Bryant Howroyd is the founder and chief executive of the ActOne Group, a global employment and workforce management company. She is a multimillionaire, a philanthropist, and the first African American woman to run a billion-dollar business. Yet when she describes some of the key challenges in leadership, she points out that her gender and ethnicity were considered barriers for potential clients:

> I'll tell you candidly—and I'm not proud of it—there were times when I would gift my intelligence to other members of my team and have them go in and make a presentation or them make the pitch so that the client wouldn't have to interact directly with me as an African-American or as a female.[11]

She concludes,

> Perhaps the one decision I would change in my career would be that I would forgive myself for being smart and being female a lot sooner.[12]

Have I forgiven myself for being a smart woman? Have *you*?

Have I forgiven myself for being a smart black woman? When I heard Howroyd's interview, I'd never thought about it that way. Yet I know there have been times when it's been easier to minimize my skills and accomplishments, when I've hidden my intellect and pretended I don't know what I actually know. To publicly own my gifts and skills seemed like publicly inviting rejection and criticism. Worse, it felt like arrogance and pride. Apologizing for my voice has come at a cost. When I've not fully owned my voice, my influence, I've squeezed myself into roles that don't fit me and don't serve anyone well. When I minimize my credentials, I negotiate in accordance with my *perception* of someone's acceptance, not in recognition of my personal worth and value and contribution. I'm poorer—literally, in some cases—for it.

HAVE I *forgiven* MYSELF FOR BEING A SMART WOMAN?

Worst of all, there is a cost to my integrity. When I'm living a lie to keep the peace, to keep others comfortable, to not rock the boat, I am still living a lie.

I've spent years in every chapter of my life—single, dating, married, a mom, a leader, a pastor, a small-business owner—silencing myself, wondering what would happen if I used my voice. I also wonder how much time I've wasted wondering what *might* happen. What I needed to consider was the heavy price I was paying by not using my voice.

Your voice makes a difference—in the trenches, to the timid, in the trauma and the triumph. Your voice in all its fullness is powerful and brimming with potential. You don't need to apologize for it or be afraid of it. But you do need to discover it, or recover it, and learn how to use it in all its beauty and purpose.

REVIEW AND REFLECT

Have you ever felt as though your voice was too much or not good enough?

What is the what-if that stops you from using your voice?

Voice Lessons

(And When to Listen to Your Coaches)

*It took me quite a long time to develop a voice, and now
that I have it, I am not going to be silent.*

—MADELEINE ALBRIGHT

Your voice has real potential. I hope this doesn't sound rude, but
have you ever considered voice lessons?"

I wasn't offended at all. My former youth pastor had left me a note
of praise and penned these words in his message after I'd performed a
solo.

The event had gone wonderfully well, and I promise you I was
not pitchy! I understood what he was saying, and I was encouraged. I
had sung informally for years, and it wasn't the first time he had heard
me sing. But on this occasion, he saw potential worth investing in.

Instead of feeling insulted, I welcomed the idea of vocal training and took lessons for singing and speaking for years. As my voice changes, I'm likely to do it again. I've learned it's one thing to find your voice; it's another thing entirely to own it. When you own your voice, you recognize its value and potential. You look after it and protect it from damage. You invest in its growth and development so it can be an effective tool.

Your *voice,* in the fullest understanding of the word, is powerful. It has real potential—for encouragement, for strengthening people in life's trenches, and for tangible influence for good in the world. And we have permission—actually, a commission—to use it.

YOUR *VOICE* HAS real POTENTIAL—FOR
ENCOURAGEMENT, FOR STRENGTHENING
PEOPLE IN LIFE'S trenches, AND
FOR TANGIBLE INFLUENCE FOR
GOOD IN THE WORLD.

Yet even when we have grasped the fact that we do have voices that God wants us to use, it doesn't mean we automatically know how to do so. If you've been silenced for years or you're used to silencing your-self, your reluctance to use your voice doesn't slip away overnight. There's a mind-set shift required, maybe even some healing that needs to take place. There's learning to familiarize yourself with the sound of your voice, and learning to use it. There may be old habits that need to die and new habits you need to form.

For some of us already using our voices, we may still need to learn how to use those voices to their fullest potential. Our voices may need further development.

Your God-given voice is worth investing in so that you may realize its potential. You may need voice lessons of a different kind. I've had a total of four vocal coaches over the years. Looking back, I realize they taught me not only vocal technique but also key lessons on living and leading with my voice, unapologetically and freely.

LESSONS FROM MY VOCAL COACHES

Let Go of the Old and Let Yourself Learn the New

I met my first vocal coach, Corinne, during my freshman year of college. Standing next to each other, we made an eclectic pair. While I was dressed by my college-student budget in old Levi's jeans, Doc Martens, and a weathered leather jacket from a thrift store, my backpack overstuffed with books and papers, Corinne looked sophisticated in a long camel-colored wool coat with a matching purse. She had rich auburn hair styled in a neat, precise bob and blue eyes that sparkled. My lessons took place in her home by her piano. Classically trained, she coached opera singers and sang arias. Her spoken voice was sweet and light, yet when she sang, I was struck by her sheer vocal power, strong and beautiful, occasionally fierce. How did my sweet, neat, camel-colored-coat-wearing coach sound like *that* so effortlessly?

My first lesson with her was diagnostic. After listening to me sing a piece, she noted how I would push my voice and strain it. Over the years, I'd formed habits and patterns that worked for the time being but would hurt my voice long term. If I wanted to develop my voice, I'd need to leave behind my old ways of singing and lay some new foundations and habits, which would feel alien at first, or frustrating and mundane, but ultimately would strengthen me and develop me. I was grateful but disoriented. It was humbling to discover how much I had to learn. I'd need to stand differently, think differently, breathe differently. We discovered habits I didn't even know I had! It took time, effort, and practice, but I learned. In time my voice grew stronger and healthier and I discovered an entirely new vocal range.

Corinne's diagnosis spoke to my life too. These years were my first away from home, when I began to reflect upon my childhood and the events that shaped and defined me. The big wide world I'd longed to make my mark on was also a scary and lonely place at times that I didn't feel fully prepared for. I'd formed habits and patterns that worked to a point, but I could tell they were beginning to limit me. For example, my way of building relationships—or *not* building them—would hurt me long term. My way of processing pain—numbing it by any means necessary—would hurt me long term.

I'd need to learn how to live differently, build new habits, if I wanted a life that realized its potential.

When it comes to your voice, what are the old ways of functioning that you need to let go of? What patterns and habits actually damage your voice and its potential?

One of the foundational skills I learned from Corinne was how to breathe, the same way endurance athletes need to learn how to breathe. My vocal power came from a completely new place once I learned where to pull the air from. In developing my influence, I'd relied on the wrong things for strength and success, such as improper breathing techniques. I've relied on old habits forged by old wounds and old stories.

My voice has been powered by my feelings, opinions, preferences, and talents. There's a place for those things. But when I'm having a vulnerable day, needing the approval of others, or when my voice is required and I'd prefer to be silent, I need to be fueled by something more substantial and weightier than opinions and preferences. Otherwise, before I know it, I'm silencing and shrinking myself, holding back all over again. I also need to be sure my voice isn't rooted and founded on the damage in my own story; it's important to clear the emotional and mental debris that stands in the way of our callings and lead from a place of wholeness. (We'll explore this topic later.)

I'm reminded that in the Bible, the Spirit of God is often described as breath (see Ezekiel 37:1–14; John 20:22). As I live and lead and speak in every sphere of my life, my continual prayer is that I will be empowered by the healing, fiery, convicting, truth-telling Spirit of God.

The other foundation that Corinne laid in my life was to expect that using and developing my voice involves work, the hard work of practice and singing scales. I had to show up and practice whether it felt exciting or not. Scales are not always fun, yet the training transforms us.

As you develop your voice and calling, consider what skills you need to develop and grow. Do you need to study, get a coach, and take courses and classes that will develop your skills, and so enrich your God-given voice?

Remember We Need *Your* Voice, Not Your Version of Someone Else's

I was in my midtwenties when I met Gwen. My college days were over, and it was a matter of working, investing in my calling, and building my adult life. I started working at my local church, and for the first year, I felt like a fraud on a daily basis. My favorite band, the Brand New Heavies, had an album track with a line that went, "Why are you such a FAKE!"[1] and I heard it in my head most days.

If only I had the skills and gifts and personalities of some of my peers.

Gwen was the director of a community gospel choir, an incredible soloist, and a vocal coach for singers and public speakers. We met in her living room. Gwen knew how to cultivate and encourage those in a community to use their voices in all their distinct beauty, so she could tell immediately that, though I was breathing well and doing all the basics, though I was using *a* voice, I hadn't quite found *my* voice yet.

I wanted to sound like my favorite artists. I wanted to sound as smooth as Anita Baker, as deep and soulful as Toni Braxton, and have the vocal genius of Whitney Houston. I wanted to sound like anyone who I felt sounded better than boring old me. And the "sound" I idolized wasn't in my range or a natural fit. Gwen challenged me gently one day to try to embrace my own voice rather than see it as a limitation, and I burst into tears.

In the weeks and months that followed, Gwen coached, nurtured, mentored, and encouraged me to allow my voice to come out, choosing pieces that suited who I actually was rather than who I aspired to keep up with. And I was better for it, not only in singing but also in how I viewed every aspect of my life.

Einstein once said, "Be a voice, not an echo."[2] One of the challenges in uncovering our voices is that we allow ourselves to be who we actually are. To live and lead and contribute to the world just as we are. It's understandable that we sometimes assume only the voices deemed popular are the ones worth listening to and that we shape our voices in their images (or again silence our own). It's as though our contributions—the way we lead, raise kids, negotiate, create art, serve—aren't valid if they're not in the same form as those celebrated around us.

It can be a challenge to discern where inspiration crosses over to unhelpful copycat imitation.

I recommend asking some of the following questions to help you uncover your voice. Not every question will be relevant. See which ones lead you forward in uncovering your voice, or use them as a springboard to the question you really want or need to ask yourself.

- Inspiration is still an important place to start, but to ensure you don't become an echo, dig a little further. *Who inspires you and why?*
- You'll find your voice at the core of your values, the things you stand for, the passion you won't let go of. *What change would you like to see in your world, work, community, family, and society? What do you think should be done to make the world around you a better place?*
- Take a moment to reflect on your childhood, what you wanted to be when you grew up. *Where are your child-like dreams, signposts to your identity and purpose?*
- Another way to uncover your true voice is to remember who you were before life, people, and expectations interrupted or invalidated you. *What would you say or*

*do differently if you were not afraid of failing or of what
people might think of you?*

- Think about your personality type. *What tools and
resources might help you understand how you're wired?
Myers-Briggs Type Indicator, StrengthsFinder, Ennea-
gram, DiSC Profile?*

- Consider your skill set, qualifications, and experience.
*What are you good at? How would you describe your
accomplishments?*

- Imagine someone gave a speech about your life's
work and accomplishments. *What do you hope they'd say
about you? What would you want your legacy to be?*

- Gwen saw and valued something in me that I couldn't
see in myself. Then she constantly affirmed who I was
until I believed her. *What do the trusted voices in your
life say about your voice and potential?*

What are you learning about your voice?

Don't Be Afraid of Your Passion or Your Vulnerability

When I met Bill, I wasn't looking for singing lessons. It had been years
since I'd sung anywhere beyond my own bathroom! I was now married, a mom, living in the US, and working with churches and organizations around the country. I wanted to sharpen my public-speaking
skills and attend to my particular weakness of talking too quickly for
my US audience to understand my firmly English accent. Bill worked
with actors and professional speakers, so I figured he'd know what
to do!

For our session, he asked me to share some of my story, something meaningful. He wanted me to talk directly to him, but as though I were speaking to a crowd. It felt weird acting like a public speaker while addressing only one person with a camera and in an industrial warehouse, but he was the expert. So I told him a story about my father, our estranged relationship, and its eventual healing. When I was done, I awaited Bill's verdict and felt strangely embarrassed and exposed.

"Jo, you don't need to work on talking slowly," he began. "You need to let yourself feel the words you have to say and the story you're telling. You'll find when you let in how you feel, you'll talk slower."

Even when I left the room, I knew that although Bill was speaking about my voice and diction, God was speaking to me through Bill's words—to speak to the bigger picture of my influence and engagement in the world around me. His words disoriented me.

I'd worked hard to regain my voice, inside and out, over the years, to talk in the trenches, to own my influence. I'd worked hard to face my fears with competence and skill and polish (all valid) so I could own a room when I needed to (amplify my voice, advocate for myself and others). I'd pushed past the voices (or songs!) in my head calling me a fake. I'd worked through the conflicting feelings that emerged when my children were little and I was trying to understand my own professional ambitions amid the endless joy of watching *Sesame Street*. I'd developed valuable skills and insights from every community we'd lived and served in. Now I wanted to move forward, and fast.

Still, I knew leadership wasn't always like that: fast and furious. The words were like touch on a tender wound. Much as I hated to admit it, any lessons learned and wisdom won happened on a bumpy, complicated path. I didn't like thinking about how hard it had been. When I first spoke in public, I shook with nerves, and my words were incoherent. When I first shared a meaningful or creative idea with a mentor or boss, I mumbled the words in case my ideas were dismissed. I recalled team meetings where I furiously blinked back tears or suppressed anger because I didn't want anything to undermine being taken seriously. I fumed in silence when I watched my ideas being presented by someone else as their own, then celebrated.

WHAT DOES IT *look* LIKE IN YOUR WORLD TO USE YOUR VOICE AND INFLUENCE WITH VULNERABILITY?

I didn't like to think about how lonely leadership had been when I was the only woman in the room. I didn't like to dwell on how hard it was to admit my own mistakes and the accompanying feeling that I was letting my gender and race down. I didn't want to think about how I'd been hurt by people in both my professional and personal lives. I'd worked through challenges, and finally I was moving into increasing opportunity. Now I wanted to be efficient and excellent. *Don't resurrect my daddy issues, Bill. And don't talk to me about feelings. Just teach me to talk slowly. That's all I came here for.*

I didn't want to be seen as weak, nor did I want to revisit any painful memories. I never thought hiding my own vulnerability and weakness could be an impediment to my influence and impact. Until I met Bill.

His lesson was an invitation to allow vulnerability to play a role in my influence rather than see it as incompetence or weakness to speed past as quickly as possible. It challenged the notion that I needed to have it all together—a clear vision, a polished, robust strategy, an assurance of success before I used my voice. Instead, I was reminded of how simple and raw stepping into one's God-given influence can be, a commission to use the words of activist Maggie Kuhn to "leave safety behind. Put your body on the line. Stand before the people you fear and speak your mind—even if your voice shakes."[3]

Don't anesthetize your passion. Don't devalue the vulnerability you feel when you lead. Don't dismiss your vulnerability, your emotion, your tears as a sign of incompetence and disqualify yourself. Your voice doesn't need to be polished; it needs to be real, raw, and brave. And present. Besides, your vulnerability is a gift to your influence because as research professor Brené Brown said, "Vulnerability is the birthplace of innovation, creativity and change."[4]

Whether it's in public speaking or in any other leadership sphere, I'm still learning to use my voice in a way that is slow enough to feel. It always feels like a risk—I still get annoyed with myself when my tears fall during a talk or in a meeting. I wish they would behave! But making space for my vulnerability in all its forms has made me a healthier, more honest leader. It's increased my reliance on God for strength, courage, and faith instead of depending on my misguided stoicism. It's deepened my relationships with people around me as our shared stories have created greater empathy and connection. We have one another's backs for our hard and tender days. And in the public sphere, when I've slowed down to communicate vulnerable parts of my story—whether it's my daddy issues, or something else (so many issues!)—my voice has given others permission to be vulnerable about their lives too.

What does it look like in your world to use your voice and influence with vulnerability?

Learn How to Focus Your Voice for Maximum Impact

I'd just turned forty when I met Hanne. When I'd gotten over the shock of how quickly the time between twenty and forty had passed, I realized I stood on the cusp of possibility and opportunity. I'd known loss and tragedy and experienced joy and love. I'd seen the impact of walking in my God-given influence, and it thrilled me. So as I hit this particular milestone, where I felt I had a bit more freedom and stability as a family, I wondered all over again what I could do with my life, how I could change my world for good.

Hanne and I met at a speaking conference. Knowing she had coached many of my friends, I asked if she had any vocal tips for me. She noted that I walk around a lot when I speak and simply recommended, "Once in a while, stop and look at one person, talk to them, address them. Imagine yourself in a conversation with them. Focus on the one."

Focus on the one.

There are so many ways we could influence our world for good. It's sometimes overwhelming—all the passions in our hearts, ideas in our minds. We don't know where to start. It would be all too easy to try to do everything and live so fleetingly that we accomplish nothing.

Hanne's words ground me when I think of words such as *influence.* They remind me of Deborah, who, long before she led a nation to victory and liberation, focused on the one in the trenches and the traumas of his everyday life. Deborah spoke courage and purpose into one man who would be a warrior, and her encouragement and leadership gave him courage to lead.

So, applying Hanne's advice beyond my work and into my life, I've learned that while I'm working through the twists and turns of big-picture dreams and ideas, I should pay attention to the one. To the people I'm in life's trenches with every single day. What might it look like to own my voice there, to have conversations that speak love and life and truth and courage? So I'm learning to pay attention to the barista or the person at the checkout at the grocery store. I'm focusing on my children, my husband, the kids in car pool, my friends and family. I'm thinking of my colleagues and their whole lives, not just our work lives. It's not that big dreams are shallow and unimportant; it's just that there are meaningful opportunities in our everyday relationships too.

Start with one. Look the person in the eye and use your voice there.

Final comment: My voice and influence have changed over the years, in expected and unexpected ways. I realized that you don't have to sing one note with your voice for the rest of your life. Who wants to sound like a flatliner? No, I've learned our voices are designed to sing arias and anthems. There's a journey to it. Our songs have texture and cadence. We whisper softly in some moments; we crescendo in others. The main thing for us to remember is that in every part of the songs, we need to show up and use the voices we've been given.

Even if they shake.

REVIEW AND REFLECT

Which one of my vocal coaches (Corinne, Gwen, Bill, or Hanne)—
and the lessons learned—do you most need to help you own your
voice?

Perhaps you're uncertain of your voice and calling and you wonder
what your voice sounds like. To help uncover your passions and skills,
imagine that years into the future, an event is being held in your honor,
celebrating your life's work and accomplishments, and then answer
these questions:

> What would your most significant relationships—spouse,
> child, parent, close friend—say about you?

> How would your team describe your gifts and skills?

> What would your colleagues say you had done with your
> time, and what would they say you had accomplished?

> How would others describe your legacy and influence in
> your world?

How to Grow Your Grit

(It May Not Be Exactly How You Think)

Fall down seven times, stand up eight.

—JAPANESE PROVERB

It was the letter Timothy had been dreading. Paul had been imprisoned for his faith before, but this was under Emperor Nero. Timothy and Paul both knew where this would end. Timothy knew Paul would write, to call for a visit or to in some way say goodbye. Timothy wasn't ready to say goodbye. Not yet. He'd known Paul since his teens. He'd grown up around him. There was so much they could still do together. The churches still needed him. *He* needed him. Timothy also felt the rising pressure of expectations. Yes, there were other leaders, but Timothy knew that in Paul's absence, many would look to *him*. He wondered if he was up to the task. He glanced at Paul's words, reading:

I think of your strong faith that was passed down through
your family line. It began with your grandmother Lois, who
passed it on to your dear mother, Eunice. And it's clear that
you too are following in the footsteps of their godly example.
(2 Timothy 1:5, TPT)

Timothy smiled as he remembered the two most significant
women in his life: his mom and grandma. He closed his eyes. He
could still hear their voices, teaching him, encouraging his own faith.
He remembered their smiles and sadness as he first traveled with Paul,
especially his grandmother, who knew she wouldn't see him again. Yet
it didn't stop her from cheering him on. Paul had filled Timothy's faith
with vision and adventure, but even Paul knew where it began. Eunice
and Lois had given Timothy a strong foundation. His life's work began
with their influence.

Tears ran down Timothy's face—for Paul, for his mom, and his
grandma. He was still afraid for the future, but he also knew he had
the strength to face it. His mom and grandmother had been preparing
him for moments like this all his life.

Timothy opened his eyes, focused on Paul's letter, and read on.

———

Timothy was a highly regarded young man full of promise and potential when he met Paul. He became Paul's coworker, writing a number
of letters with him, planting faith communities in Philippi, Thessa-
lonica, and Berea. Like Paul, Timothy was imprisoned for his faith (see

Hebrews 13:23), and historians note that Timothy went on to become the bishop of Ephesus, dying in AD 97, likely a martyr.

By the time Paul wrote his final letter to his protégé (see 2 Timothy), Timothy wasn't a new leader on a daring adventure anymore, nor had he reached the stage of the sage bishop over what was arguably the most significant region for the church for the first few hundred years of Christianity. Timothy was somewhere in the middle: the time when he had discovered his strengths as well as his weaknesses. Timothy had encountered some victories but also some defeats. And now some painful goodbyes.

> GRIT HAS *Two* COMPONENTS:
> PASSION AND PERSEVERANCE.
>
> —Angela Duckworth

As Paul wrote to prepare Timothy for the days ahead, he focused on the young man's growth as a leader. He reminded Timothy of his identity and his faith, his purpose and calling. He wrote candidly of others who had lost their way. Paul urged Timothy to be proactive about his own leadership development and purpose.

"Train yourself to be godly." (1 Timothy 4:7)
Throw yourself into your tasks so that everyone will see
    your progress. (see 1 Timothy 4:15)
Keep a close watch on how you live and on your teaching.
    (see 1 Timothy 4:16)

"Guard what God has entrusted to you."
   (1 Timothy 6:20, NLT)
Fan into flames the spiritual gift God gave you.
   (see 2 Timothy 1:6)

Paul recognized that God's grace surrounded and undergirded Timothy, but the young man was not a passive participant on his journey. It required active engagement, active development, and active resistance to anything that might inhibit or undermine Timothy's calling. It required diligence and endurance. If he was going to come out on the other side of this challenging segment of his life, he was going to need grit.

> **grit:** noun
>   (Entry 1 of 2)
>   1 a: sand, gravel
>   b: a hard, sharp granule (as of sand) *also:* material (as many abrasives) composed of such granules
>   2: any of several sandstones
>   3 a: the structure of a stone that adapts it to grinding
>   b: the size of abrasive particles usually expressed as their mesh
>   4: firmness of mind or spirit: unyielding courage in the face of hardship or danger[1]

When Angela Duckworth—academic, psychologist, and author—explored the drivers behind success, her research led her to conclude that the idea of success being solely shaped by talent was woefully limited. Instead, her research uncovered that grit played a huge role. Duckworth stated that "grit has two components: passion and perseverance"[2] and believes that growing our grit has the power to help us realize our potential.[3]

Grit is an essential ingredient for living into your purpose, I've discovered, but it's not one I've always wanted, or wanted to need! Throughout my own journey, I've hoped for some magical moment when I felt suddenly and supremely brave. When I would somehow emerge with the confidence and courage to say all the things I yearned to say, to be all the things I wanted to be, and to make all the sacrifices I needed to make. I've longed for that silver bullet that would instantly transform me into a focused, passionate woman of influence. Alas, my reality has proven itself to be something quite different from my much-preferred fairy-tale narrative!

When my family and I relocated from Southern California to Minnesota a few years ago, we exchanged our walks along the beach for walks by one of many lakes, our year-round moderate temperature for landscape-transforming seasons. I loved seeing the fall again, but I was intimidated by the thought of a Minnesotan winter.

Winter comes to Minnesota for an extended stay and can turn streets into sheets of ice. It's not for the faint of heart. Collecting my mail from across the street becomes a mammoth task with slow, deliberate steps; the occasional slip precedes a desperate fight to remain on my feet and save myself from hurt and humiliation. I'm five foot nine, so it's a long way down!

I have definitely discovered a new appreciation for grit. Our icy climes require that we regularly grit our streets, roads, paths, and driveways. And not just a bit of grit either; we need lots of it, scattered liberally on our paths. When it's worn through, we scatter it all over again. Our ability to safely move and function depends on it. Now grit is an integral part of my winter, both the sand-and-gravel kind that helps me move around and the psychological kind as we wait for spring to finally break through.

Grit makes all the difference. However you live into your influence, whatever way you hope to make an impact on your world, you will need grit for the journey. To keep your feet firmly planted on your path, you will need to recover the meaning of underused words like *endurance* and *perseverance,* and delicious old-school words like *gumption* in your life. You'll need tenacious courage to keep going on the road when people don't want to hear your voice or receive your influence and your confidence is slipping. You'll need the determination to unwrap your gifts, even when life tells you to hide them all over again. You'll need the resolve to maintain vision and focus, to keep walking when the terrain is punishingly hard.

HOWEVER YOU LIVE INTO YOUR INFLUENCE, WHATEVER *way* YOU HOPE TO MAKE AN IMPACT ON YOUR WORLD, YOU WILL NEED *grit* FOR THE JOURNEY.

Though our journeys vastly differ from Timothy's, we too will need to heed Paul's advice to be proactive participants in our leadership development, adopting habits and practices that will cultivate and grow our grit. We'll need lots of it.

HOW TO GROW YOUR GRIT

The good news is that transformational growth is possible. The honest news is that there is no magic wand to get us there. But here are a few things we can do to grow our grit, and they all start with the letter *R*.

Rest

"Don't make your moves when you're tired or exhausted. The margin for error is too great. Rest is a weapon. Don't forget it."[4]

If grit is about keeping going even though you want to give up, where does rest fit into that? I've learned in distance running that my rest days are an integral part of my training. If I push too hard all the time, I'm more susceptible to injury and burnout. Intentional periods of rest build resilience, give me time to recover, and renew my energy for the trails.

The same is true for our whole lives. We need intentional periods of rest to help us recharge, to help us keep going for the long term. An example of this would be taking a weekly day off.

We might see a day off as an antiquated (and slightly sanctimonious) religious ideal that has no place in today's fast-paced world. Bethany Morgan, a Messianic Jewish believer and executive director of a global ministry (and a mother of two), offers a different perspective:

> When the Lord gave people Sabbath, He was redeeming
> and giving His people freedom. It's a gift to His people.
> When they were enslaved, they didn't get rest; they didn't
> get to operate with a time frame or a calendar. They had no

control over their bodies or their time. God restored to them—Sabbath, rest, a time frame—because they were not slaves; they were His people. One of the amazing things Sabbath does for me is that *whenever I struggle to take a Sabbath (a day off), it reminds me to take a look at what holds me captive.* Because the most important thing about Sabbath is that I am free to rest, I am free from control, and that the Lord of the Sabbath is my Lord, and so I can worship and rest for that day because I am not enslaved; I am the free child of a King. I'm not a slave to the work, or to the world.[5]

If we *cannot* stop and rest, what is holding us captive? Sometimes our challenges are external: the nature of our employer or immediate supervisor, the challenges of getting out of debt, or holding down more than one job while carrying the weight of the responsibilities at home (more on that later). We still need to explore what rest might look like for us, because burnout and breakdown will jeopardize the lives we long for.

Rest is a weapon. Don't forget it.

Renew Your Thinking

"Don't copy the behavior and customs of this world, but let God transform you into a new person by changing the way you think" (Romans 12:2, NLT).

We know now that the way we think determines the way we live and lead. Our thoughts and thought patterns have the power to ignite our purpose and set it ablaze. They also have the power to completely extinguish our dreams and limit our actions. To keep our thoughts strong enough for the paths we're called to, we'll need to exchange the narratives that can derail us for ones that propel us.

When I'm feeling negative about my voice or my influence or my impact, I need to take my mind off myself and regain perspective. One way I do this is through practicing thankfulness. I'm struck by how often I've heard the stories of business leaders and corporate executives who adopt a gratitude practice, journaling what they are thankful for on a regular basis.

My gratitude practice often revolves around prayer, thanking God for who He is and all He has done. Thanking Him for the big and the small things I've often taken for granted. It lifts my spirit. It reminds me that any leadership roles I take are in response to His loving call and that I depend on His guidance and power. It gives me the strength for the challenging parts of leadership and the courage to withstand difficulty because I'm already thinking of a bigger picture.

Is it possible to change your mind? Well, yes. A recent neurological study has revealed that our brains are affected not only by our genetic makeup and our negative and positive experiences in childhood but also by our adult experiences, practices, and choices.[6] In short, the apostle Paul was right: whatever our current mind-sets and patterns, there is hope that our minds can be renewed and transformed.

Rebuild Your Heart

"Guard your heart above all else, for it determines the course of your life" (Proverbs 4:23, NLT).

One of the definitions of *grit* is "unyielding courage."[7] It's interesting to note that the word *courage* comes from the Latin word *cor,* which means "heart."[8]

The state of your heart affects your grit for the journey, so it's no wonder you're advised to guard your heart; the stakes are high. Still, to guard it is not a call to isolationism, nor an excuse for emotional distance or lack of transparency. On the contrary, it's a call to be proactive about those things that shape who you are, such as your character, experiences, and wounds.

Don't wait for someone else to tell you to get your heart healthy. Don't wait for your significant relationships, colleagues, employers, or clients to tell you to heal your heart. Don't let the damage you've received on your path determine and derail your life. Remember there is One who "washes your feet."

It takes grit to acknowledge heart damage, and healing that damage is one of the ways you can grow grit. It might require vulnerable conversations and prayer times with trusted family members or friends. You might benefit from a period of working with a therapist. But you will be rebuilt and have the capacity to stay on your path and not be knocked down or manipulated by every challenge, success, or disappointment that comes with the territory of walking into purpose.

Remember Playtime

"As you go about the hard work of your career, it is critical to remember to play."[9]

When I was in elementary school in England, recess had another name: playtime. No more reading and trying to write in cursive, no more math. No more sitting in front of the school's sole huge desktop computer (the eighties, friends). It was playtime. Fun for the sake of fun.

The work of influence and purpose can be all-consuming. It can even occupy our minds way after we have officially stopped working. Especially when work is on our smartphones, one email away! When every waking hour is dictated by our tasks, our progress, and our roles, we will eventually be drained physically and emotionally. We become one-dimensional beings because we've forgotten to play and have fun.

Whenever I'm under pressure at work or when leadership becomes difficult, the first things to go are the things I do for fun and enjoyment, the things that bring my soul back to life. Instead, I resolve to push through. *I'll play when all the work is done,* I tell myself.

Except work is never done. Unless I draw a boundary line, I'll never stop.

It's been vital for me to recover the things that bring me back to life and receive them as gifts that God has given me to simply enjoy. I've needed to learn to enjoy the life I've been given and the beauty that surrounds me and give myself permission to love the things that restore my soul. No other agenda required.

And for the hardworking, purpose-pushing people among us, it's important to highlight the benefits. In their essay "Cognitive Fitness," Professor Roderick Gilkey and Dr. Clint Kilts note that "in adult life, play engages the prefrontal cortex (our most highly evolved and recently acquired brain areas), nourishing our highest-level cognitive functions—those related to incentive and reward processing, goal and skill representation, mental imagery, self-knowledge, and memory, just to name a few. Play, therefore, improves your ability to reason and understand the world."[10]

It's time to recover that neglected hobby, to join that choir, to take that walk, to try out that new restaurant with friends, to visit that art gallery. Play makes you stronger. Play grows your grit. You've worked hard; now it's playtime. Fun for the sake of fun.

WHEN IT'S NOT ABOUT GRIT AT ALL

Growing grit and resilience is important, but it's also incredibly important to note when the situation we face is about something bigger. Sometimes we've internalized messages from our experiences that tell us it's healthy to tolerate situations that are dangerous, even abusive. Worse, sometimes we are told it's holy to do so. We know well enough to advise someone else against it but somehow reason it's okay, important, or purposeful for us to grin and bear it. Here are some examples.

Issues Around Your Mental Well-Being

It's one thing to count your blessings and write in your gratitude journal after a long, frustrating day. However, if you are experiencing depression, anxiety, panic attacks, or suicidal ideation, you need to take a different course of action.

Many of us feel so ashamed of the issues surrounding mental well-being that we suffer in silence. Maybe talking about these issues is not a conversation we are used to having in our homes and friendship groups. Maybe we avoid admitting our issues to ourselves because we feel it would disqualify us from greater influence and opportunity, and we mistakenly think we should be stronger. Grit is not the answer here; you've suffered long enough. Please seek the help of a doctor or therapist, because they are trained and equipped to help you on your journey.

Sexual Harassment

It's been chilling to hear the stories of the #MeToo movement—the abuse of power and trust, the violation of women's bodies while their careers, professional opportunities, or academic grades were held to ransom. Yet it's not surprising. An online survey conducted by Stop Street Harassment found that 81 percent of women and 43 percent of men stated they had experienced some form of sexual harassment in their lifetimes.[11] The span of the definition included verbal harassment, unwelcome sexual touching, unwanted genital flashing, and sexual assault.[12] So many of us have suffered in silence and shame.

If this is your story in your workplace or in your community, what happened to you was wrong and not your fault. If this is your story in the church or in your home, what happened to you was wrong and not your fault. Grinning and bearing it is not the answer. No matter what you've been told, enduring the abuse, minimizing its impact, and blaming yourself for it is not the "Christian thing to do." It's time to tell your story to someone who can guide you toward the best next steps for your protection and freedom.

Toxic Work Environments

You're consistently overworked and underpaid. You're taken for granted. You're useful to them, so you are used. Your gifts, your skills, and your talents are consumed, with little recognition, and it leaves you wrung out. There's a difference between deploying your gifts for a team effort and having your ideas stolen and someone else claiming the credit. It's just that it's happened to you for so long now that you're unsure which is which. You spend your days listening to sexist and racist diatribes, and you can tell who views you through the lens of their own stereotypes. You're tired of being bullied; you're tired of feeling afraid of your employer.

Our lives are complex, so there may be valid reasons as to why we've endured toxic work environments (as well as toxicity in our friendship groups or in our relationships) for so long. But it is time to explore how to address the toxicity. Do you need to pay a visit to HR? Do you need to search for a new job? Sometimes the healthiest—and, dare I say, *grittiest*—response to work environments like that is to leave.

———

A final word on growing your grit: remember why you're doing this, and keep going! "Our visions are the world we imagine, the tangible results of what the world would look like if we spent every day in pursuit of our WHY."[13] Everybody wants to give up at some point. When that happens to you:

> Remember the vision that burns in your heart and mind. Write it down somewhere so you can remind yourself later when the path is unclear.
> Remember your talents, the skills and the wisdom gleaned through life, that you can contribute and serve others with today.
> Remember why you're leading. Remember your faith and the people you're sent to serve: your family, your community, your city, your company. Remember your *why;* it'll remind you to grit your path.

And keep going. One foot in front of the other. It might not be as fast as you'd like—it might even be a slow crawl—but you're moving. Keep going. Let us remember the words of Timothy's mentor, Paul: "I admit that I haven't yet acquired the absolute fullness that I'm pursuing, but I run with passion into his abundance so that I may reach the purpose that Jesus Christ has called me to fulfill and wants me to discover" (Philippians 3:12, TPT).

Keep. Going.

REVIEW AND REFLECT

Which of the *R* ideas do you need to work on right now to help you grow your grit?

What could you do in the next twenty-four hours, week, month to help you develop in this area?

In what part of your life do you realize that it's not about grit at all but something else?

Choose the best person to talk to about growing your grit and together come up with a plan.

Body Talk

(And How to Listen to What Your Body Is Saying)

I'm learning that both body and soul require more
tenderness and attentiveness than I had imagined.

—SHAUNA NIEQUIST

How did I get here?

It began as an ordinary, unremarkable day. My husband went to
work, and my kids went to school. It was our normal morning routine:
loud, organized chaos. My mother-in-law was visiting and had seam-
lessly woven her way into our family patterns, her presence making
everything easier. It was an ordinary day. Except for one thing.

I ignored it at first, the strange pace of my heart. Beating differently, pacing strangely, faster than usual. I ignored it because I was

busy. I ignored it because I didn't want to know. In a nanosecond, I decided this was the best and most appropriate course of action. I'm a Brit, so I keep calm and carry on because it's in my bones, it's in my blood, and it's exactly my cup of tea.

It was there again the next day, a peculiar irregularity—faster, harder, asking to be paid attention to, refusing to be ignored. So I ignored it *harder,* forcing my newfound theory that I could will it away. My mind over this matter. I had things to do, other things to think about.

We reached the third day, my heartbeat and I. Beating weirdly, pacing strangely. It wasn't asking for attention anymore; it was insisting, demanding an audience. So on the afternoon of the third day, I called the doctor's office to see if it was normal.

When I told the receptionist my reason for calling, she referred me to a nurse immediately. He asked me questions, lots of questions, questions that made me nervous. When I'm nervous in medical situations, I tend to tell jokes to make the medical team laugh. It's my way of telling them, "You need to tell me this is okay." (It also passes the time, like when I was induced with my firstborn and was told I couldn't move because they discovered I had preeclampsia. All I could do was lie in bed, eat ice chips, and wait for the oxytocin to kick in. Fourteen hours later, they broke my water to get things moving—*Wait, is that your personal knitting needle?* Hilarious.)

The nurse told me to ask my mother-in-law to take my pulse. Slowly and deliberately, he said, "I want to bring you in right now, but I've checked and all our doctors are fully booked. I need you to go straight to the nearest urgent care and tell them what I tell you."

When I got off the phone, I packed some snacks and a few books, and we made our way to the local urgent care. I explained to my mother-in-law, who was confused by my behavior, that the word *urgent* in *urgent care* was, in my experience, more of an aspiration and faint hope than a reality, so we might be there some time. I'd found urgent care to be an excellent opportunity for some "me time" in the past and was sure this would be no exception.

It was the speed at which the urgent-care center got me in that scared me. They asked about family history, and I forgot to answer. They told me I needed an EKG, and within minutes I was in a robe, in a bed, with multiple electrodes attached to me, wired to a machine monitoring me. After all the phone calls, snack gatherings, chatting, form filling, and question avoiding, I was suddenly alone. The room was empty, and I was left wondering what was going on with my body, listening to beeps and finally paying attention, close attention, to my heart. The attention it had been trying to get for three days now. The room was white, sterile, and cold. No windows. I started talking, first to God, then to myself. *I know I'm not going to die, but is this how I want to live? How did I get here?*

The doctor came in and spoke: "Good afternoon, Mrs. Saxton."

I smiled (a little harder than needed) and extended my hand to shake his (I have a firm handshake). My British keeping-calm side said as brightly as I could, "You can call me Jo."

"I've looked at the report . . . *Mrs. Saxton.*"

Okay, then.

"So your heart is fine, but clearly something is going on. We need to get to the root of what is causing these palpitations."

There were more questions, more answers. I relaxed, but I was still nervous, so every time he called me Mrs. Saxton, I kept smiling and giggling, insisting, almost pleading, that he call me Jo. He didn't relent, not once.

Then the doctor asked, "How do you sleep?"

"Well, I slept in February," I responded. I'd stopped giggling and delivering one-liners at this point, but I kept up the forced bright smiles.

The doctor paused, stopped writing, put down his pen, and then looked at me.

"Mrs. Saxton, it's October."

The game was up. I didn't try to smile anymore. I couldn't even hold his gaze. I looked down and studied the cold white floor.

"Yes," I said, nodding. "Yes."

"Insomnia. I think we've found out why you are having heart palpitations."

Insomnia. The word had a certain gravitas when it came from his mouth. A gravitas and a truth. I decided not to name it. I'd simply concluded I didn't sleep well, had a bad night or two, tossed and turned a bit.

For seven months.

"It's been a turbulent year."

He continued what he had to say and strongly recommended an appointment to see my usual doctor as soon as possible. He'd send his notes over to my doctor's office immediately. He reached out and shook my hand, looked me in the eye, and said, "Take all the time you need before you leave."

"Thank you."

"I wish you well, Mrs. Saxton."

I was alone again in the sterile white room, asking myself two questions:

Is this how I want to live?

How did I get here?

I pulled the electrodes from my body. I got dressed and folded my robe, slowly, delicately. I smoothed the bed down as my emotions finally caught up with me. There was no room for my stoicism or passionate strength. I felt vulnerable and I knew it. My strangely pacing heartbeat had tried to tell me, was still telling me. This time I wasn't going to avoid it; the silence in the room wouldn't let me. My head hung low and I took a long, deep breath. I needed to admit to myself that I'd not slept since February. I needed to face something. I needed to face a lot of things.

How did I get here?

Is this how I want to live?

I took one long last look at the room. I wanted to remember it, how empty and official it was, how cold the electrodes felt, how afraid I was when I didn't know what was wrong, how powerless and vulnerable I felt. I wanted to remember that it was this moment, in this room, that I asked, *How did I get here? Is this how I want to live?* I locked the image in my mind. I took it in deep, sure of one thing: I would find out how I got here and decide how I wanted to live, because I didn't want to return to a room like this anytime soon.

The answer to how I got to a place where insomnia gave rise to heart palpitations and a trip to urgent care is, like life, layered. Time, distance, and healing seem to nuance my answers and understanding of that day. Still a number of things were pretty clear.

There had been an earth-shattering experience in my professional life, and I hadn't seen it coming. I was in a job I loved and found deeply fulfilling. I loved the team I worked with and was part of a community I loved and enjoyed. It was more than a job to me; even our families were connected. If I wasn't living my best life, I certainly felt like I was moving in that direction. In truth, it had healed some old professional wounds and scars. My heart was full, and I looked confidently toward the future.

I didn't know that during that time, my picture-perfect world wasn't real. Looking back, I wonder if I saw only what I wanted to see. Maybe my wounds needed the job to be a success. Did I use my dreams to enhance my reality? Perhaps the tremors were there and I simply ignored them. Then a tsunami hit the job I thought was a perfect fit, leaving a desolate, decimated landscape. It fractured my friendship group, wounded our family, and broke me.

And then—silence.

I slept in February. I didn't sleep in March. Or in April. By May, I didn't expect to. My nights were interrupted by moments when I woke up in a cold sweat, retracing my steps, reliving conversations. Or when I tossed and turned, my mind on overdrive. Thinking was exhausting, but not exhausting enough to help me sleep. I wept and worried about the future, worried about our finances, our plans for our little family. There would be no new house now. I worried about my kids and the potential upheaval in their lives.

Some nights I lay awake because my heart mumbled prayers when words wouldn't cut it. Other nights I lay awake simply because I was angry and raw. I may have been silent during the day, but the twilight hours heard every single word I had to say.

Then there were the worst nights, the most terrifying nights, when I'd wake, gasping for breath, reaching desperately for air, yet paralyzed by fear or panic or maybe shock. It was like waking up into a nightmare. It happened three or four times in a night. I dreaded going to sleep, so I'd stay up late at night, watching TV. I begged for it to stop. Not only did it refuse, it increased, until it was happening on a nightly basis. Three or four times a night. Until October, when one morning I woke up and noticed the strange pace of my heart.

At my follow-up appointment at the doctor's office, my physician went through my records. He asked about my sleeping patterns and then said, "Mrs. Saxton, looking at your history, it seems you've put on quite a bit of weight recently, in a short space of time. Perhaps we should check your thyroid?"

My eyebrows arched and I replied, "Doc, you can check my thyroid, but I'm pretty sure it's fried chicken."

There was no point pretending. Without warning, the surge of emotion welling up in me burst its walls. "It's been a horrible year. I'm sad, I'm not sleeping, and I don't know what to do. Every day is stressful, and when I'm stressed, I eat. All I do is eat."

I'm not sure either of us was ready for that confession, especially my reserved Minnesotan doctor. This was not how our appointments worked. They were extremely practical and informative, punctuated by the invitation to call me Jo, which he consistently ignored. Now my keep-calm-and-carry-on attitude had been carried off somewhere, and in the awkward silence that followed my vulnerability, vomit emerged. I wondered if getting a pap smear would be more comfortable. Trying to gather some composure, I said with *especially* English annunciation, "You'll be relieved to know I am indeed in therapy."

I left his office with a prescription for anxiety and an appointment for tests. My thyroid was checked, and I later learned my diagnosis was 100 percent correct.

When I recognized that my body was giving voice in some way to my heart, my emotions, and my mind, it was obvious what had brought me here:

Trauma, shock, and grief.
Job loss, loneliness, and mounting bills.
Words and accusations lodged in my mind.
Shattered dreams, broken relationships.
Layer upon layer of years of disappointments.
My tendency to carry on tenaciously, ignoring my
    limits.
My broken method of taking care of everyone else in
    crisis but *me*, just as I always did.
The realization that things were out of my control, and
    out of control, period.
The thought of starting all over again at forty, unexpectedly,
    when I didn't want or plan to.

All those things and much more brought me here. I shouldn't have been surprised. It was only a matter of time before I would realize I wasn't invincible. But then I'd been ignoring my body for years until I had no choice but to pay attention.

———

A Conversation, in Theory

The women had gathered. I opened the envelope and began to speak. "So I'm going to read the question, and you say the first thing that comes to mind: 'If your body could speak words, what do you think it's saying to you?'"

Amber laughed. "I think I saw this on Pinterest. 'You are not in college anymore. For the love of God, woman, eat a salad.'" Everybody laughed with her. She asked, "Is that what you were looking for?"

"Quite possibly," I replied, "though sometimes I've had to make sure I'm distinguishing between what my body is saying to me and what the mirrors in my house are saying to me."

Seeing their confusion, I carried on. "They might tell me to try a salad or, more often in my case, to remember my veggies for very different reasons. My body says it because I love vegetables but don't always make time to prepare the food I love. Instead, I settle for something more convenient, less healthy, and often less satisfactory. Yet whenever I make the time, the food is great and my body feels amazing.

"Then there's my mirror. It holds a very different standard of beauty, health, and desirability than my Nigerian heritage. When the mirror tells me to have a salad, it's sneering. It's disgusted with my soft, full stomach, my dimpled thighs, the lack of definition in my arms. It is telling me I look unacceptable. It berates me for the last cookie I ate, and it reminds me I will never be attractive enough to be worthy.

"So as you think on this question, be aware that the mirror

might want to talk to you, but listen to what your body is actually saying to you. It might relate to food, but it might be something else entirely. Does that help?"

"That's exactly what I needed," said Amber. "I've spent years listening to the mirror and the magazines, following every fad, failing, and then fat shaming myself for weight gain or the lack of a dramatic weight loss. I love the idea of learning to listen to what my body is saying. I think she wants to be liked and not punished."

Angela smiled, then wryly offered, "I hear you, Amber. My body would say, 'You beat the eating disorder from twenty years ago, but it's time to admit your eating is *still* disordered. And you exercise too much.'"

I smiled as I saw Angela step out in vulnerability. I knew that it cost all these leaders to open up as they had in recent weeks. But I'd noted it was particularly challenging for Angela. She was breaking out of the mold that her career path had often de-manded of her: strong, cold, distant. The tender honesty was good to see. It made her stronger.

Kate added, "Mine would say, 'Drink more water. Dehydra-tion makes you mean.'"

Bree shared, "It would say, 'Admit why you don't sleep. You tell people your kids kept you up, but your worries do, especially about your finances and about your husband's job.'"

Rachel shook her head. "'Stop criticizing everything about me all the time. Treat me better. We're on the same team!'"

They went on, adding things like:

"You've been running on empty for years, and you're
   about to hit a wall. This time I won't get up so
   quickly. Please stop."
"My body would say, 'Eating to numb your pain isn't
   working.'"
"You're avoiding the doctor's routine checkup again.
   Make that appointment."
"My body would tell me, 'You're neglecting what I need.
   I need time. Real rest and space. Tender care. You
   treat me this way because you feel unworthy. I can't
   keep up with your need to keep everybody happy.'"
"You've been feeling low for months, but you always
   reason it away. It's time to talk to a professional
   about it."

Then we sat together in silence for a long time.

—————

WHAT IS YOUR BODY
TRYING TO TELL YOU?

I invited a gathering of women leaders to complete a survey. Some of
the questions were fun and silly, such as "How many of you are wearing the wrong-sized bra?" (90 percent). Other questions went deeper.
One question asked if they felt they were close to burnout—76 percent of the women said they were. These were women of different
generations and life stages. Different ethnic and cultural backgrounds.

Leading in churches, businesses, nonprofits, and their local communities. Women with significant influence and purpose, nationally and internationally. Yet there they were, on the edge of burnout, their bodies crying out with exhaustion.

Is this how they wanted to live? Of course not. Nobody consciously chooses acid reflux and sleepless nights. Nobody wants to work constantly, rest rarely, or wake up more tired than he or she felt the night before. Nobody—including the many women I've coached and the woman I see when I look in the mirror—ever wants to live that way. Nobody wants to be defined by their hurts and hang-ups, their wounds and weaknesses, or someone else's.

They were driven there by hanging on, pushing through, and carrying the emotional weight of being overlooked and underinvested in while carrying out their roles and responsibilities. Some were worn down by perfectionism because they felt it was required in order to climb the ladder at work. They knew that when they walked into work, they didn't just represent themselves. Like it or not, they were seen as a representative of all women, or of all women of color. There was no room for error, because a sister would suffer or not get an opportunity as a result. They needed to show up and not mess it up for anyone else. No pressure? No, all the pressure.

They knew they needed a regular day off. They believed in a Sabbath, but weekends were spent catching up on the weeds that had grown up in their lives when they were busy working. Or they felt they had to perform on the weekends too, perhaps leading in a different capacity than the workweek demanded, but they were still "on." They were driven there by narratives that said they need to be everything to everyone at all times. By stories that said they should be grateful for the chance to get to lead at all. They were holding down a few jobs to cover debt and that time the car broke down and cost a fortune to repair. No one had told them that to neglect their body was to neglect and wound their soul.

YOU HAVE ONE BODY, AND *your* LEADERSHIP LIVES IN IT. IF YOUR BODY COULD *speak,* WHAT WOULD IT SAY TO YOU?

This is not how I wanted to live, but I didn't feel I had a choice. So I led and I pushed and I proved, while doctor's appointments told me I was stressed out. It took time to think that a different way was even possible. Was there a way to exist in the world I lived in without it driving my values and so defining the rules by which I functioned as a leader, as a human being? I couldn't wait for the world to change on my behalf. I had to start taking responsibility for my own body and well-being rather than keep meeting the consequences of when I didn't.

You have one body, and your leadership lives in it. If your body could speak, what would it say to you?

If you're not sure how to listen to your body, here are a few areas to pay attention to:

- What are your sleeping habits?
- When was the last time you took a vacation, had a day off, or did something you enjoy?

- What are your eating and drinking habits?
- How does your body respond to stress and pressure?
- How well do you keep routine doctor and dental appointments? Mammogram, anyone?
- What makes your body feel its best?

A Practical Plan, Rooted in Your Everyday Life

When I left the doctor's office with a prescription and follow-up appointments, it was only the beginning. Therapy continued for a number of months. There was a renewed commitment to exercise and watching what I ate, and most importantly, I committed to going to bed at a decent hour and resting.

One of the things I rapidly realized about listening to my body was that it's not a onetime event. While I've not returned to the emergency room with heart palpitations, my body has spoken loud and clear about the stresses and strains I've forced on it on more than one occasion. It has reminded me of my need for rest, renewal, and nurture.

When I'm looking out for other people, I forget all too easily what I need to do for myself. It's an area of my life that is a weakness, and I'm acutely aware that it's where I need people looking out for me, ensuring I'm listening to what my body is saying and doing something about it.

I need people who will love me enough to cheer me on and love me enough to challenge me when needed. And I don't just need that for a body talk, but in every area of my life.

Everybody does, including you.

REVIEW AND REFLECT

What is your body saying to you?

What will you do about what your body is saying?

What is your plan for this week, this month, this year?

The Search for Community

(And All the Things That Stop Women from Having It)

The success of every woman should be the inspiration
to another. We should raise each other up. Make sure
you're very courageous: be strong, be extremely kind,
and above all be humble.

—SERENA WILLIAMS

"We need to talk. All of us. Together."

"We can't do it here."

"I know, *achoth.*"[1]

"We can't do it now either."

"No. We'll leave early in the morning, and we'll go to the edge of
the camp, where the women are. We'll be left alone there. They'll assume we are on our monthly cycles."

"All five of us, at the same time?"

"Have you ever known a man to ask for such details? Trust me, sister. They will not question us."

Five women, all sisters, quietly made their way to the edges of the camp, past the families and tribes they'd lived among for years. They weren't normally this closed and secretive, hidden from their community. Yet they all knew this conversation would trouble even their closest of friends.

Eventually, far away from the remote possibility of eavesdropping, the women sat down—Mahlah, Noah, Hoglah, Milkah, and Tirzah. Sisters. Daughters.

Noah started the conversation.

"Sisters, our father was a good man, the best. But he is gone now. His passing leaves us vulnerable. We are not married, so there are no men to cover us. It's harder now. Every family will receive property as their inheritance in the Promised Land. Our father would have received property. But now he is gone, and we stand to receive nothing. Why should we be punished when we haven't done anything wrong and he hadn't done anything wrong? And make no mistake—it will be a punishment. We will be destitute. We know what happened to Mahlah's friend Rachel and her mother when her father passed."

Mahlah sighed heavily and wiped tears from her eyes. "They had no money, no resources, no safety. Those men, those evil men who promised to look after them, did so at a cost. They have used her body, and they have broken her. She will never be married now. She will never belong. Even the women in her tribe despise her. As though she had a choice."

Noah continued, "Sisters, it isn't fair. And it won't be fair for us either. I think this census is our opportunity to be heard, to be counted. We need to make our case. We need to ask for our inheritance."

Hoglah spoke next. "Will the heads of our tribe do anything for us? Will the clans even remember us now that Father is gone? The only one who can do anything about our case is Moses."

"Then it's Moses we need to speak to," said Noah, "and we need to do it in front of the whole assembly, for everyone to hear."

Tirzah gasped. "Noah, are you serious? We are nobodies in this community; we are *nothing*. We have no warriors in our family. We are not Levites. The clans from our own tribe won't even think of us. Everyone is so sick of this desert that all anyone cares about is finally getting his own land. I've heard some of the men talking. If we don't have land, they get more.

"So why would anyone think us even worthy of speaking to Moses in front of the assembly? Moses talks to *God*. He doesn't speak to *us*. We'll get in trouble for this, and people will not forget. They'll think we're thieves and troublemakers trying to steal the land they want to give their children."

"I think what Noah is saying," began Milkah, "is that we're in trouble anyway. And if we don't do anything, it will get worse."

Noah nodded as her sisters began to comprehend the severity of their situation. They were vulnerable, but they also seemed powerless to do anything about it. It was overwhelming.

Tirzah began to cry. "I'm scared, so scared."

"So am I," said Milkah, squeezing Tirzah's hand.

The women huddled together and held each other tightly.

"I'm scared too," said Noah. "And I don't think I could face Moses by myself. I certainly couldn't speak up about this alone. But I'm not alone in this. There are five of us. We are living this together, going through this together. Maybe we can be strong for one another. We've made it through the wilderness and gotten this far. We have lived through difficult times, mourned both our parents, and soon we will be out of this terrifying place. Since our father cannot be with us in person, at least let his name be there in the inheritance, the property he wanted to give to his children. We must do all we can to ensure that this Promised Land that our people dreamed of, that our parents could only dream of, is a promise of hope and life for us too. And who knows? Maybe also for the Rachels of our community."

"I agree," said Mahlah. "We can do this together. We'll take turns and say what we need to say."

"We'll go to the tent of meeting," said Milkah. "Tomorrow?"

"Yes," replied Noah, her confidence rising. "Tomorrow."

Would Moses listen to these women? Could they change the status quo? Here's what happened next:

> The daughters of Zelophehad son of Hepher, the son of Gilead,
> the son of Makir, the son of Manasseh, belonged to the clans
> of Manasseh son of Joseph. The names of the daughters were
> Mahlah, Noah, Hoglah, Milkah and Tirzah. They came
> forward and stood before Moses, Eleazar the priest, the leaders
> and the whole assembly at the entrance to the tent of meeting
> and said, "Our father died in the wilderness. He was not
> among Korah's followers, who banded together against the

LORD, but he died for his own sin and left no sons. Why should our father's name disappear from his clan because he had no son? Give us property among our father's relatives."

So Moses brought their case before the LORD, and the LORD said to him, "What Zelophehad's daughters are saying is right. You must certainly give them property as an inheritance among their father's relatives and give their father's inheritance to them." (Numbers 27:1–7)

It's hard for us to fathom the strength and courage the women needed for this formidable moment. Women without male relatives were vulnerable during this time. Without a male support system, they could end up destitute, with only the option of prostitution as a means to provide for themselves. They stood before Moses, their great leader, and Eleazar, their priest, because they had to. They had no choice but to stand before their entire community and advocate strongly for themselves and one another, making a huge, unprecedented demand. It wasn't that their request hadn't been made before; it hadn't even been thought of before. Zelophehad's daughters were pioneers, trailblazers—not by passion or dreams but by sheer necessity.

Moses listened to the women and sought God for wisdom. God told him that the women were right, so Moses not only granted Zelophehad's daughters their request but also made it a law for any woman in a similar position to them. They changed the fabric of their society for themselves and for the women in their community from that point on. They made history.

When I look back on my life and my journey in leadership, I realize that my relationships have served as powerful catalysts for growth, maturity, and opportunity. People have invested in me, stretched me, challenged me, encouraged me, stood with me, listened to me, created opportunity for me, and opted to be led by me.

There have always been other people around and actively involved in my life, up close, and in my business from an early age. I inherited the large extended family of immigrants that my parents met in the early years of establishing their lives in the United Kingdom. Many were from the same Yoruba tribe, with a shared language, traditions, and practices. Others were from tribes within Nigeria or beyond.

IF YOU WANT TO GO *fast*, GO ALONE. IF YOU WANT TO GO FAR, GO TOGETHER.

—African proverb

I didn't have *one* mother; I had *mothers*. It was a loud and vibrant blessing unless I was in trouble. When I was in trouble, my mum would send me to see them all—Aunty Bassey, Aunty Margaret, Aunty Olive—for advice, instruction, correction, and some occasional nagging. But Christmas and birthdays and other special occasions had awesome potential because I had mothers and aunties and uncles and cousins. So many cousins!

Therefore it was part of our way of life that you wouldn't ever make a pot of rice for just yourself (or even just a few people). You didn't know who was coming around, and there needed to be enough for everyone and extra to take home. It also meant that, regardless of the size of your apartment, *everybody* was going to live with you (much to my chagrin), for some time at some point in some way.

Family was never defined as "nuclear" (at least not in its size). It always extended, it was *a lot,* and I still miss it.

———

It's a largely Western phenomenon where the primary understanding of "family" was who you married and who you gave birth to—the nuclear family. While the nuclear family is often credited with offering greater independence, mobility, and economic opportunity, people also reflect on the cost. Novelist and software engineer Nicole Sallak Anderson states that for all its benefits, the nuclear family "has also isolated us, creating situations where many adults are lonely. Whether stay-at-home parents, single moms and dads, or even the elderly in nursing homes, we have paid a price for the pretty little cages we call home."[2]

When we look at cultures and communities in the Bible, again we see the extended family in action. Jesus described His followers in familial terms (see Matthew 12:47–50) and prayerfully and intentionally selected people for that group. Later in in the New Testament, *oikos* is the word used to describe a household formed by blood and non-blood ties. The oikos was also a center for community and business life and launched the first leaders of the fledgling churches in the Graeco-Roman world.

Author John Coleman remarks, "Some of the greatest accomplishments in business, politics, and culture have come not from individual initiative alone but from those working *in, with,* and *for* community."[3]

As the African proverb goes, it takes a village to raise a child. I believe it also takes a village to raise a leader. It takes a village to nurture, sustain, and propel a leader forward. It takes an oikos and extended family, a community, a friendship group, and a sisterhood. A range of people with a range of gifts, skills, insights, and investments to make in a leader's life in myriad ways. When we've built villages around our leadership and lives, we accomplish far more than we could ever hope to accomplish on our own.

WHEN WE'VE BUILT *villages* AROUND OUR
LEADERSHIP AND LIVES, WE ACCOMPLISH
FAR MORE THAN WE COULD EVER HOPE
TO *accomplish* ON OUR OWN.

Living and leading with purpose is a collective work. At its most basic, functional level, the concept of a village sounds beneficial. Who wouldn't want the support of a village of people? Functioning at its best, it sounds like the healing, transformative antidote for our climb-to-the-top leadership.

Why does it almost seem like a radical and countercultural idea, then?

THE GREAT (WO)MAN THEORY

Scottish historian Thomas Carlyle once said, "The History of the world is but the Biography of great men,"[4] believing that divine inspiration and heroic types with distinct and unique qualities shaped culture and history. The Great Man Theory, as Carlyle's influential idea on leadership came to be known, modeled leadership through an individualistic and personal lens. And while history does reveal great men—and women—who played significant roles in culture-shaping events, a closer study of their lives reminds us that most often there were other people involved, sharing the weight of purpose and sacrifice with them.

At school I learned about the work of British abolitionist William Wilberforce and his campaign against the evils of slavery. But I didn't learn much about the group he worked with (the Clapham Sect) or the other abolitionist movements working toward the same goals.

I grew up learning of Nelson Mandela and Archbishop Desmond Tutu, and their anti-apartheid activism. It would be years after that initial introduction to these incredible leaders before I learned more about the movement they were part of. The hero's narrative is remarkable, but it's incomplete without the story of that person's remarkable surrounding community.

We might not have heard of Carlyle or thinkers like him, but we've certainly been influenced by his worldview. We've seen examples of his idea of the individualistic leader in art and film, in the heroes and superheroes we admire. Or we've grown up in or have been heavily shaped by a cultural backdrop that emphasizes and celebrates the accomplishments of the individual without the story of his or her community.

Consequently, we conclude that the effectiveness of leaders is solely based on their personal charisma, preternatural talents, popularity, and gifts, as well as grace on their lives. It's as though these leaders have the "it" factor, something unique and indiscernible, even magical. Unable to compete with this limiting, truth-distorting perspective, countless leaders are left isolated and feeling inadequate.

When I meet women leaders, many describe the loneliness and isolation that have defined their journey. It's the most common conversation I have when I'm talking to a female leader. Sometimes the isolation helped grow grit for that leader, but even when it did, too often loneliness had a debilitating effect on her energy, her vision, and her ability to serve.

These women are tired of going it alone, wearied by the accompanying limitations. They want to explore what going *together* might look like. What it would be like to see leaders like them in the room with them, in meetings, in leadership positions above and beneath them. To *not* be the only one.

> To be part of a network, a tribe, a village . . .
> Surely it would be easier, more encouraging, more fun?
> It would catalyze our purpose in new ways.
> Surely it would be transformative from the inside out, right?

Yet I've had many conversations with women leaders who suggest that building a village of relationships isn't always straightforward or nurturing. We've experienced competition with our peers and other leaders; we've encountered gossip and alienating cliques. We've had to compete or been compared, and neither has helped build safe relationships. Sometimes we've done the comparing. We're not proud of it, but it feels inevitable somehow. We feed off the feeling of being "better" than someone else and drown in the realization that another leader possesses skills or opportunities we don't have.

Other working professional relationships were beset by jealousy and envy. Our progress presented a problem, a threat. Our careers were sabotaged to make the problem go away.

A village? When our experience feels less like Zelophehad's daughters working together and more like the Plastics from the movie *Mean Girls,* of course we'll back away from the idea. Going alone feels safer.

And still, for some of us, there is no major backstory behind our lack of villages. It's simply something we've not experienced, because:

> We've moved a lot for work.
> We're the only woman or one of few women leading
>   in our context.
> We don't have time or context to make friends.

Whatever our experience and perspective to this point, our relationships still have positive roles to play in shaping and catalyzing our leadership. We need them to realize our God-given potential. Some relationships may already be in our lives, simply underutilized. The rest we'll need to learn how to build.

But first things first. We need to learn to identify and dispose of cultural barriers and personal debris that stand in the way of laying the solid foundations required to build villages.

We'll need to identify and dismantle our personal version of the Great Woman Theory. Never mind the tired trope of whether a woman *can* or *should* have it all. Who defines what the archetypal *all* is for women—of different socioeconomic groups, ethnicities, life stages, ages? Meanwhile, back in everyday life, beyond the theories and think pieces ("Yes, she can!" "No, she can't!" "Maybe!" "Sometimes!"), we're still wrestling the everyday actual *all* that we have to deal with in life and the *all* that we expect of ourselves. If, expanding on Thomas Carlyle's idea, the Great Woman Theory is part of our worldviews, we won't build villages, because as leaders, we're supposed to possess all the talents required for history-defining impact.

Do it all. Be it all. Have it all. Know it all. Live it all. Try it all. Work it all. Give it all. Love it all.

Prove it all. Carry it all. Make it all.

And, of course, be incredibly successful in it all.

The Great Woman Theory is exhausting, because it's all too much. No wonder it's hard to show up in leadership and potential when we don't know how on earth to make them fit into our already over-burdened, stuffed lives. If we can't be the Great Woman of God we feel we should be, we back off from opportunities or harshly criticize ourselves, mistakenly believing that we're the problem. That we're inadequate to respond to God's call. That we're clearly not enough.

You weren't made for leadership in isolation. It's a work that takes a village of support, sustainability, and resourcing. It simply cannot exist inside one woman's life (or one man's, for that matter), even though that's the biggest lie we've been told.

SCARCITY—ROOM FOR ONE

Another pernicious and pervasive belief revolves around the idea of living with a scarcity mind-set and facing a scarce environment. It emerges when we don't see any women coming through to positions of influence. Most often it emerges when we see only one woman (occasionally two) leading among a group of men. It seems there's room for only one woman in a leadership position, one woman at the decision-making leadership table, one woman of color with a prominent role. Whether intentional or not, the presence of only one woman in a leadership position at a time communicates that there's room for only one woman, one expression of leadership, one set of gifts.

This reality can leave women leaders in a quandary. When there's only one seat available at the table for a crowded field of qualified women—and that seat provides not only professional fulfillment but also economic advantages that have huge implications for the woman and her family—of course it gets difficult. How do you generously share inside info about that rare professional opportunity that could get you out of debt, pay off your father's medical bills, support your child through college, or help you overcome that significant money issue that has been out of reach? What happens to notions of sisterhood if it could cost you a chance at career advancement or any type of career at all?

When there's room for just one, you are automatically pitted against another woman. Comparison is inevitable. Unhealthy competition is the norm. You sense the only way to fulfill your purpose is if she doesn't fulfill hers. If you want to move at a different pace or have different goals, that's fine, but what if you're looking at the same kinds of opportunities?

Some business and thought leaders challenge us to step away from a scarcity mind-set, which dictates our thoughts and self-worth and ultimately our actions. In his article "The Scarcity Fallacy," executive-leadership coach and columnist Bill Carmody contends that "this feeling of scarcity is the big lie that we all have bought into. It is this innate fear that rests deep inside of us, whispering to our subconscious mind that we simply don't have enough."[5]

Entrepreneur and author David Meltzer urges leaders to exchange the scarcity mind-set for one of abundance. In his article "Belief in More Than Enough: Abundance Mentality in Business," he wrote, "Abundance is created by believing that you live in a world of more than enough."[6]

Still, the data on women in leadership argues that their world doesn't have enough room for them. In the US alone, while women account for 50.8 percent of the population,

- when it comes to leadership positions—such as law partners and medical school deans—women account for no more than 20 percent;[7] and

- the world of the arts is just as problematic for women. As actress Viola Davis noted when speaking in direct reference to her industry, "The only thing that separates women of color from anyone else is opportunity."[8]

Indeed, the stats on gender disparities—in leadership roles and also in pay differences—could go on for pages.

So while I'd agree with the *concept* of abundant opportunity for all of us, the data (and the stories of the women I've known) reminds me of that concept in George Orwell's *Animal Farm* where everyone is equal, but some are more equal than others. The abundant opportunities are not equally available or equally distributed, even when we believe we are enough. Even when we know what we bring to the proverbial leadership table. Systemic patterns of gender and cultural bias through our communities can create a scant landscape of scarcity for women.

To that end, it's no wonder a scarcity mind-set and worldview emerges among women when they are trying to fulfill their passions and their callings. When the scarcity issue is real and complicated, it only adds to our isolation.

NAVIGATING THE MENTAL LOAD

"Behind every great man is a great woman," the saying goes. It's been noted that the phrase became popular in the 1940s as an acknowledgment that a man's success was not the result of the Great Man Theory after all but instead often had a lot to do with the woman in his life—usually his wife, who dedicated her life to her husband's success.

I've heard this phrase used a few times when a husband is expressing deep respect and appreciation (sometimes tearfully) for his wife in a speech. He mentions how his wife's sacrifices (sometimes of her own career goals), her dedication to raising their children and managing their home, her adapting to and organizing relocations, and her attending to the needs of wider family created room and capacity for him to excel in his career and rise to positions of leadership.

Yet if today's women leaders were to give a speech, while they'd undoubtedly acknowledge their partner's support and influence, would the details of their stories be different?

A United Nations study discovered that women do 2.6 times the amount of unpaid labor that men do.[9] An investigation by Bright Horizons of the work-and-life habits of today's families found that despite all the professional advancement of women, in addition to the rigors of work and career, women still carried "the mental load" of their wider life: dealing with the household, children, and extended family needs to a far greater extent than their husbands.[10] Sixty-nine percent of working moms said the household responsibilities create a mental

load.[11] Fifty-two percent said they were burning out from the weight
of their household responsibilities.[12] And before we blame men and
husbands for everything, the study learned that working husbands
and fathers also felt immense pressure and observed that attending to
family needs was deeply frowned upon at work.[13] How can they afford
to take a stand on behalf of their families if it costs them the professional advancement that pays the mortgage, covers the bills, and con-
tributes to supporting their family's needs?[14]

How are we supposed to handle the reality of our mental load? Of
household commitments, of dedication to children or older relatives?
Where do calling and purpose fit into that? It's evident the mental load
has taken its toll on our mental health and our physical well-being. It
burdens our relationships with our spouses, with the potential to breed
confusion and resentment. It reminds us that doing it all can come at
a heavy price.

Perhaps we'd assume that navigating the mental load would mean
we would be more open to drawing in help and support. That is, until
you place it alongside the Great Woman Theory, the scarcity problem,
and deeply ingrained cultural beliefs about the roles and capacities of
men and women. The Bright Horizon study documented that while
89 percent of Americans believed that working moms in leadership
brought out the best in their employees, 69 percent believed they were
also more likely to be passed over for a new job.[15]

Placed alongside these other pressures, conquering the mental
load can become a badge of honor, a sign of success and having it all
together. Until it collapses. Until we get heart palpitations and our
vices numb us and there's no one to talk to—really talk to—because
we've done such a good job of performing the role of a confident, suc-

cessful Christian woman that we don't have the words to admit we are desperately lonely.

TIME TO LIVE A DIFFERENT WAY

The Great Woman Theory, the scarcity issue, and the mental load have the potential to crush us if we truly believe that rising into our leadership means we should do it all. It's not just the biggest lie of all; it's the cruelest too. There has to be another way, and there is. We need villages of life-giving relationships to rise into our leadership. As you already know, they aren't easy to come by. We will need to build them brick by brick—over days, weeks, months, and years. It's hard work, but it will strengthen your leadership, and sometimes it just might save your life. It's time to build your village.

REVIEW AND REFLECT

Have loneliness and isolation affected your call to leadership? In what way?

When do you feel the pressure and expectation to be and do it all?

Which of the barriers to community—the Great Woman Theory, the scarcity issue, and the mental load—pertains to you the most and why?

11

How to Build Your Village

(One Brick at a Time)

We are better leaders when we are rooted in a community
empowered to counsel us, challenge us, and hold us accountable.

—JOHN COLEMAN

The concept of building a village is not merely a matter of busying yourself with lots more people in your life. That would be exhausting and unappealing. Besides, you can be surrounded by people and still be the loneliest person in the room. To build a village is to recognize that to grow as a leader, you need to actively attend to specific types of relationships that help you flourish. Broadly speaking, two types come to mind.

First, there are the relationships that give you "roots." These are the relationships that provide the environment you need to ground your life and stay whole and connected. These are the relationships where you feel known, where there is trust, and even though such relationships can be vulnerable and have challenges, they feel safe.

MEANINGFUL RELATIONSHIPS ARE NURTURED THROUGH *openness* **AND CONNECTION, FORGED THROUGH CHALLENGE AND DIFFICULT CONVERSATIONS, AND DEEPENED OVER TIME THROUGH THE SPONTANEOUS MOMENTS AND** *habitual* **HANGING OUT.**

Then there are the relationships that give you "wings" and help you soar into your potential. Like the roots relationships, they invest in you, but they often take a different form. These relationships help create and provide opportunities, often leveraging their time, talent, and connections. Relationships that give you wings help you fly in your influence and impact. These people might share insights with you, offer you opportunities, and train you and sharpen your skills.

Which relationships give you roots?
Which relationships give you wings?

When we examine our relationships, we might find that some fall into both groups or have even moved between the groups over the years, and that's normal. We also might find that one type is more comfortable for us to develop and enjoy, while the other type is awkward and difficult. Maybe sit with that a minute, explore why, and begin to work on those weaker relationships. Meaningful relationships do not just happen overnight. They are nurtured through openness and connection, forged through challenge and difficult conversations, and deepened over time through the spontaneous moments and habitual hanging out. They are fused by common values and shared missions.

Most of the relationships explored in this and the next chapter will be familiar to you. Some of your relationships may not have been utilized in the ways suggested in this book, some might feel vulnerable to engage in, but they are essential for your growth.

So to get the most out of these chapters, treat them like diagnostic tools to help assess the village you've built and are building. As you look at "roots" (the first of these two types of village relationships), try this exercise:

- Observe how the examples make you feel. Do you feel tension? Pain? Hope? Take note of what they ignite or inspire in you.
- Add more relevant examples to each type that specifically reflect your own life and leadership where needed. Don't be limited by the examples given here. Write the names of the people who come to mind.
- Acknowledge the relationships needing some work or help.
- Finally, simply knowing the roots you need is not transformative in itself. You'll need to create a plan to build your village. With that in mind, pay close attention to habits and practices that glue these building blocks in place, and, as needed, add your own.

Let's begin by exploring some building blocks for the relationships that give you roots.

SIGNIFICANT OTHERS

Who are your significant others? I'm not just talking about romantic partners here. Who are the individuals that make up the key relationships in your life? The people who know you, beyond your responsibilities? These are the people who matter to you most—whose opinions you value most—often because they know you best. They could be your closest family members and your friends.

My siblings have always been my significant others. Even though we are spread across three continents and today conduct most of our relationships through technology, there is an immediate ease whenever I am with them. They know who I was and who I am. Before I got married, my roommates and my friendship group were my key people; they were the ones who saw my life up close. Today my husband and my children occupy my primary "significant other" space. They are my heart and my home, the most important relationships of my life, and I spend more time with them than with anyone else. They know me at my best and my worst.

Your significant others are the ones who know you at your most vulnerable and will confront you when needed. These relationships ground you.

Habits that cement these relationships are found in building rhythms of connection, opportunities to be together. These moments don't always have to be expensive, but they are intentional, consistent, regular, and worth sacrificing for:

- date nights
- family time
- Friendsgiving, or other specific gathering times with friends

- day trips, weekend breaks, movie nights
- shared rituals and activities in the holiday season
- meals
- group conversations via text

This isn't quite as simple with my extended family living across three continents, yet we've found our rhythms of connection through technology in between the times we're able to get together. Also, rhythms of connection are not just for married couples, people in relationships, or people with children. Everyone needs healthy rhythms of connection in their key relationships.

One of the things that was profoundly helpful when I was single and in my twenties was having mentors who validated my need for genuine relationships and didn't equate singleness with legitimized workaholism. At work my key relationships were considered as valuable as my colleagues' who were married with children. So when work was especially busy and we were all under pressure, it wasn't automatically assumed that because I wasn't married I had more time and should cover everyone else. When my colleagues were encouraged to prioritize time with their spouses and children, I was also actively encouraged to prioritize the significant relationships in my life.

What are the rhythms of connection you need to develop with your significant others?

A WORD ON THE POWER OF FRIENDSHIPS

We need friends for every stage of life, not just "until we settle down." We need the friends who know us from the chapters of our histories, but we also need to be open to and proactive about making new friends. Naturally, you cannot be friends with everyone to the same degree, but cultivating friendships in real time remedies the debilitating loneliness that hits us leaders. Who do you do life with? Where do you go to fall apart? We need friends who will ask us, "When did you last take a day off?" "How are you dealing with that temptation?" "What are you doing about your dreams and your best ideas?" We need friends who can see how we're healing (or not). Who can talk to us about our money and our spending. People who strengthen us in the everyday stuff of life—do you have someone like this? That's what I mean by friendship.

As for habits that cement friendships, on top of building rhythms of connection, we need:

- *Fun.* Coffee dates. Lunch. Girls' nights. I've learned to value time with my women. Now, as a married mother, I've had to ensure I make time for female friendship.
- *Honest, authentic conversation.* Not just a handful of exchanged texts.
- Willingness to forge *new friendships.* It might seem odd to describe new friendships as a "habit." But when a life transition takes place (e.g., new local church, moving house, career change, a relocation across the country) or even when life gets busy, we will need to make the choice to build new friendships. Consider them another gift worth unwrapping.

Take an honest assessment. Do you have some friendships currently in an unhealthy place? How do you need to respond?

Which friendships are life giving for you? How are you investing in them?

Are you open to new friendships?

#TeamRelieveMentalLoad

As I stood at the school gates waiting for my then kindergartner, behind my smile, I was struggling. I knew I was traveling for work the next day—again. I didn't want to leave, but we needed the money. I missed my kids, I enjoyed my job, and I felt utterly conflicted all at once. So I felt guilt, the kind of mother guilt connected by a cultural ought-and-should-shaped IV inserted into my veins. I felt deep shame.

My thoughts and feelings were interrupted by my fellow school-gate mom Sonja, who said, "Hey, I just want you to know—I've got you. The kids can come to my place. I'll feed them and they can play, and Chris can come and get them when he's ready." I was caught off guard and my eyes welled with tears (probably more guilt than gratitude), and I thanked her, apologizing and explaining the guilt I felt.

Sonja grabbed my hand as if to call me to attention. She said, "Okay, so you need to understand what is happening here. You are going to fulfill your mission, and this is my mission here. My mission is helping you do what you do. Let me do my mission. I'm not called to go and do all these other things; this is what I do, and I do it really well. Let me do it. Let me look after your kids. Let me help, let me feed them if they need it, and let me be there for your family."

So I accepted her kind offer, and when I'd return from a work trip, Sonja would ask, "So how did *we* do?"

Extended family, be it your blood or your friends who are like family, can share the mental load.

Sometimes our perfectionism undermines the relationships that help deal with the mental load. Perhaps your roommates or your spouse or your kids aren't as proficient in domestic tasks as you and don't do things the way you would. *It's easier or quicker if I just do it,* you tell yourself. But doing so takes its toll on your time and energy, and it has the potential to breed resentment in those relationships.

If you let go of certain tasks and expectations, what might change?

If your family members were active participants in managing the household, what difference might it make?

Some tasks might require external help beyond family and friends. Depending on your budget and what's available in your local community, consider what job you might be able to hire someone for. Is there a teenager in your neighborhood who walks pets or babysits?

Would it help to have a cleaning service or meal service, even if only for pressured times of the year? For some of us, the idea is a relief! For some again, it challenges our expectation of ourselves as a Great Woman of God. Nonetheless, we all need to think through the practical resources that make life work rather than spiritualizing an exhausting schedule and ultimately burnout.

Here are suggestions to help you build #TeamRelieveMentalLoad:

- Remember the power of the Great Woman Theory here. What are the cultural oughts and shoulds that harass you and guilt-trip you?
- Consider the things you love to do, have to do, and would rather not do, and brainstorm with your spouse or a friend about them.

- Assess the area of greatest need in the household tasks.
- Are the people who share the household also sharing in some responsibilities? Have you taken on too much, gotten tired of asking, decided you do it "better"?
- Ask for help, and receive it when it's offered.
- Swap skills, resources, and ideas with your friends. For example, can you have a batch-cooking night with friends, where you cook a lot of food together and supply one another's kitchens and freezers with food?
- Do you have the financial resources to pay for additional support in your home?
- What can you pray for?
- What are your next steps in managing the mental load?
- Who do you need to talk to first?

FAITH COMMUNITY

Your faith community, your church, is an additional place to get rooted through groups, activities, and worship experiences. Retreats are a place for bonding, and small groups and events can forge friendship through shared passions.

Yet for some of us, trying to get rooted at church can be challenging. Some of our work roles and family responsibilities mean we can't be at church for daytime groups and evening studies. We don't have the capacity to be volunteers at the end of a long workweek. Others work for churches and are uncertain where boundaries end and everyday relationships begin.

For some, particularly those of us who resisted our call to leadership, wounds originated in our church relationships. A number of Christian women I'd met who were flying in the business world struggled deeply when it came to understanding their places in the church:

- "It's so strange. I'm so confident in my profession that even with all its challenges, I know what I am there for. But when it comes to the church . . . I just don't know . . . I don't know how I fit."
- "I don't think they're comfortable with my career ambitions."
- "When it comes to being involved in church, it feels like I can give my money but I can't give my leadership experience."[1]

Yet the church is our spiritual home.

What does it look like to be part of a place you believe in and to find a place to belong?

Is it time to find a new community, join a new group, or try again in the place you currently attend? Reengaging with your local church might not necessarily sound like a fun girls' night out at first, but it's worth persevering with. It provides a solid base for your life and leadership.

What might it look like to put roots into your faith community?

A Place to Process Pain

We already know leadership can be painful, and many of us have been hurt and scarred in the process by rejection, loneliness, and difficulty. We're stretched, tired, challenged, under pressure. But leaders or not, life has happened to all of us. We're survivors of devastating circumstances: recovering our lives after marriage breakdowns, dealing with the loss of a child or parent, getting a diagnosis no one wants, financial challenges, anxiety, and stress. Yet sometimes we expect ourselves to cope because we're leaders. We take care of everyone else—that's what we do—until somehow it becomes who we are. We push our problems to the back, until . . . *heart palpitations.*

> BUILDING A VILLAGE INVOLVES CLEARING
> THE DEBRIS AWAY AND LAYING NEW
> *foundations* THEN BUILDING ONE BLOCK
> AT A TIME. IT'S HARD, SWEATY WORK,
> AND IT'S NOT REMOTELY *sexy.* IT WILL
> TAKE TIME. BUT IT'S WORTH IT.

We need to build places in our village of relationships where we can process pain, so that our leadership and callings are not used to hide away from it. Sometimes friends and family are enough, but sometimes we may need something more, such as:

- a prayer appointment at church
- spiritual direction
- recovery groups (such as Celebrate Recovery, Alcoholics Anonymous, Grief Recovery Institute)
- a counselor, therapist, or psychiatrist

How do you currently process the pain that is an inevitable part of life?

Where do you need to go to process pain?

Take some time to consider the relationships you need in your life to ground and sustain you and the practices that cement them in place. We know it's not easy. Building a village involves clearing the debris away and laying new foundations, then building one block at a time. It's hard, sweaty work, and it's not remotely sexy. It will take time. But it's worth it.

Laying these foundations makes it possible to fly.

REVIEW AND REFLECT

Think about the different "roots" relationships. What have you learned by assessing your village relationships?

My strongest relationships are:

My weakest relationships are:

The relationships I especially need to focus on are:

This is my next step for cementing that relationship in my life:

12

The Strategic Relationships Every Village Needs

(You Might Feel Awkward About Them at First)

Cultivate a network of trusted mentors and colleagues.
Other people can give us the best insight into ourselves—
and our own limitations. We must have the courage to
ask for help and to request feedback to expand our vision
of what's possible.

—MARIA CASTAÑÓN MOATS

Our villages are vital for keeping us rooted, connected, and whole.
They break the hold of loneliness, guard our hearts, and keep us
steady. They also ensure we don't take ourselves too seriously, that we
give ourselves breaks, and that we have fun!

Then there is another part to the villages: life-giving relationships we need. These are the relationships that strengthen our callings in practical ways. In these relationships, other women train us, build us up, advise us, share their knowledge and opportunities with us, give us our breaks, elevate us, and launch us into our purpose. As beneficial as these relationships are, women are often hesitant when it comes to utilizing them.

Leadership experts Sally Helgesen and Marshall Goldsmith observed that women are concerned that when they build relationships helpful for leadership growth, they are using people, playing politics, serving their own agendas. The skill of leveraging relationships had been somehow reduced to a negative personality trait, a manipulative approach to people, or as Helgesen and Goldsmith noted, "The underlying belief that exercising leverage translates as not being a very nice person," adding, "This is problematic because leveraging relationships is key for achieving professional success."[1]

How does it feel to think your village needs to be peopled with the kind of support that gives you wings to fly into your calling? Does it feel acceptable or just plain awkward? Does it feel cold and clinical? Maybe it reminds you of all the things you dislike about the idea of networking and it doesn't feel authentic and genuine. Worse still, doesn't it feel like we're callously using people for our own ends?

Sometimes we pull back from engaging in these relationships, concluding that if God wants this for us, He'll just make it happen. We surmise that "if it's right," people will miraculously come up to us and offer their help and advice out of nowhere. However, I'd contend that even though God does move miraculously and does bring people across our paths, many of His miracles are earthed in the realities of us engaging with our callings. After all, we're not damsels in distress; we're just everyday ordinary women rising into our God-given calls. We're simply seeking to be faithful with our callings and faithful stewards with the gifts the Lord has entrusted to us. One of the ways we engage those callings is found in the relationships we're building.

Over the next few pages are examples of some of the relationships that will help you fly into your calling, along with another reminder of how to assess where your "wings" relationships currently are. As you read:

- Observe how these examples make you feel. Do you feel tension? Pain? Hope? Take note of what they ignite or inspire in you.
- Add more relevant examples to each type that specifically reflect your own life and leadership where needed. Write the names of the people who come to mind.
- Acknowledge the relationships needing some work or help.
- Finally, simply knowing the wings you need is not transformative in itself. You'll need to create a plan to build your village. With that in mind, pay close attention to habits and practices that glue these building blocks in place, and, as needed, add your own.

Let's begin by exploring some building blocks for the relationships that give you wings.

PROFESSIONAL PEERS

Ocean's 8 took a significant departure from its predecessors in the *Ocean's* films franchise. It was still a star-studded, glitzy, fun, and fantastical heist movie, but for this outing, the lineup was all women. Their characters were not girlfriends or secretaries, sidekicks or henchwomen; the women were the masterminds of a brilliantly planned heist of the Met Gala in New York.

When the film was released, the press paid a lot of attention to the relationships among the leading women in the cast. They were Oscar winners, Grammy winners, YouTube stars, wildly successful writers and producers. Did they get along? Was there tension? The cast graciously sidestepped the assumptions behind the questions, assumptions that a group of powerful women couldn't possibly be friends. Of course, these questions were rarely (if ever) asked of their male counterparts, but in some interviews, they noted the professional impact of sharing time and space with women in their profession. They talked about agents and managers, experiences and expectations.

Actress Sandra Bullock explained, "I realized there were so many questions I had and didn't know who to ask in the journey of my career. And here I sat in a room with seven other women who might have those answers. We all threw everything into the pot, and by the time we left, I felt like we had gone through college together."[2]

Our professional peers are the people who are at the same stage as us professionally. When we're trapped in competition and comparison with our peers, we're denied the benefits that conversations and collaboration can bring. If we can choose not to see those people as threats, we might discover they are colleagues, friends.

Over the past few years, I've spent a lot more time building relationships with professional peers. And as those relationships have grown, there's a brain trust developing—I even call some of them part of my "personal board of directors." Our conversations are honest, practical, and vulnerable. Our topics range from self-care to professional contacts and opportunities. We even discuss what we're getting paid. Like all good relationships, they take time and effort. But they have strengthened and sharpened me. They have made me wiser and clearer on my calling. These women are in my corner, and I'm in theirs. We celebrate one another's gifts and opportunities and success.

What cements these relationships?

- *Making room for more.* Remember the scarcity problem, the idea that there's room for only one? These habits that help build professional peer relationships confront this mind-set head on, acting in the opposite spirit. We can't always avoid or control the environment offered to us or the obstacles it places in our way, but I refuse to be defined by it. I don't want to see other talented, smart, fearfully and wonderfully made women as threats. So where scarcity is self-preserving and withholding, these habits are all about audacious generosity! Even if the landscape is scarce, I can still choose to live by abundant generosity and play my part in creating the culture I want to see.

- *Celebrating and encouraging others.* Who is out there in your world doing good work, making an impact? Who has succeeded against all odds? Who is soaring in their work right now? Celebrate them, congratulate them, and tell them exactly how great they are. Remind them of how valuable their work is in the world. And do it regularly!

- *Sharing.* There are peers who would benefit from the lessons you've learned, the conversations you've had, the people you've met. There are introductions you could

make, connections you could facilitate, advice you could
give that could propel others forward. There is help you
could receive.

- *Staying open to new relationships.* When we're not defined
  by scarcity, peers are not threats but rather opportunities
  for relationships and developing our networks of professional connections. Stay openhearted and be proactive in
  building relationships with new peers in your field. Their
  progress does not automatically mean your failure.

- *Welcoming collaboration.* Perhaps you don't have to
  undertake that project alone. Consider the people you
  can partner with to see a shared dream realized.

- *Keeping it clean when competing.* Is there ever a context
  when you *have* to compete? Perhaps it's because we've
  been burned by competitive attitudes in relationships that
  we might veer away from the idea. We rightly emphasize
  the value of collaboration, the benefits of celebrating
  others. Nonetheless, there are still going to be contexts
  where we must compete. It might be at work when two
  teams bid for the same account. It could be when you and
  a friend or colleague apply for the same position that you
  both see could change your quality of life and be strategic
  to your career trajectory and purpose. It might be tempt-
  ing to downplay your ambition or avoid the opportunity
  so as not to hurt someone else's feelings. I'm not convinced
  that men are weighed down by the same confusion about
  the inevitable reality of competing with others in order to
  fulfill their professional ambitions. If we are serious about

living into our influence, there may be occasions when we
have to learn how to compete well. In the world of sports,
we see healthy, strong, ambitious athletes who know how
to bring all their skills and training to the table but also
know how to manage the sting of defeat with poise and
grace as they congratulate one another and shake hands.
Athletes who are friends with their rivals away from the
sport. The athletes who make us cringe are the ones who
are known to win by cheating or who have a reputation to
be scathing and rude to other players. It's a good illustration for us. There are times in leadership when we may
end up competing with others for an opportunity. Don't
be the kind of leader who wins through underhanded,
manipulative means or by dragging others down, speaking poorly of them to make yourself look better. Be the
leader who gives your all to the opportunity but is honest
with others about what you hope and aim for and who
treats your competition with poise, grace, and maturity,
whether you win or not.

Still, the caveat here is that you might do all the right things and
still get used. People might be fake, defined by scarcity and insecurity,
and their actions will be at your expense. They'll work to win by ensuring you lose, badly. We human beings have a way of deeply misread-
ing, mistreating, and disappointing one another, particularly when we
succumb to our insecurities and brokenness. We'll still need to exercise
courage and wisdom as we usually do when building relationships.
The benefits of healthy professional peer relationships reach beyond
the risk.

- Who are the peers you need to build relationships with?
- How will you make room for more?
- What networks can you join or create?
- How do you process the inevitable competition that comes with fulfilling your professional potential?

MENTORS AND SPONSORS

"If I have seen further, it is by standing upon the shoulders of giants,"[3] Sir Isaac Newton wrote to fellow scientist Robert Hooke in February 1675.

I hear the cry for giants from women in leadership all the time, especially in faith-based arenas. It's a hunger to learn from someone who is further along on her leadership journey. As women navigate through the complexities of leadership, they want the wisdom and clarity that comes from someone else's maturity and experience. And if that someone could be someone like them who could speak to the added dimension of leading as a woman or something even more specific (for example, leading as a woman of color, leading in a particular career path), it would be even more meaningful, again dissipating the loneliness and impostor syndrome that affect so many of us. This is where mentors and sponsors fit in.

A mentor shares wisdom, reflections on her own experience, in a way that helps you frame yours. Over the years, I've benefited from the wisdom of mentors. One mentor taught me the importance of dealing with the pain of my past as I grew in leadership. She shared practical tips on what she'd learned to do when painful memories were triggered by helping others face their pain. Another mentor helped me work on my budget and financial goals, modeling how she made her money go further by establishing key principles in her life.

A mentor is a fresh pair of eyes, an experienced mind, an honest living example (note: *living* example, not *perfect* example—perfection is too much to expect of any human being) of healthy leadership. A mentor might be in your sphere of work, but depending on the advice and guidance you're looking for, she might be found within your wider community and beyond.

Yet in an interview regarding her essay "Why Men Still Get More Promotions Than Women," Professor Herminia Ibarra said she believed mentoring was not enough. Her research revealed that high-capacity women leaders were receiving mentoring but still not progressing in their careers as they desired. She concluded that women needed not only mentors but also sponsors.[4]

Sponsors are also established and experienced leaders who leverage their influence, trust, and credibility to get their protégés to places they simply couldn't get to by themselves. Their influence creates opportunities that can launch people forward professionally. What's the difference between a mentor and a sponsor? Simply put, as economist and author Sylvia Ann Hewlett clarified in her essay "The Real Benefit of Finding a Sponsor," "Mentors proffer friendly advice. Sponsors pull you up to the next level."[5]

As I look back over twenty-five years of various leadership positions, a few sponsors were involved in my story. They made introductions and recommendations that shifted the course of my career. These sponsors were not complete strangers; they were people I'd known for lengthy periods of time. I'd served their vision, worked on their teams, given time and energy to their work for years. They not only knew about me; they knew my work ethic and the results of my work.

Furthermore, I didn't just work extra hard in the hope of being noticed and selected. Even in the sponsoring process, I had to own my voice and take initiative. I wanted help to get to the next level, so I needed to explain my dreams and ambitions and find a way to ask for advice and recommendations.

Sharing my dreams and ambitions made me feel incredibly vulnerable at first. *What if she laughs? Worse, what if she* doesn't *and she thinks I'm a terrible person?* Besides, it was a big ask, requesting someone else to invest her reputation and currency in my calling in some way. Yet when my sponsors were at decision-making tables in meetings, they put my name forward. They leveraged their reputation to ensure I was given opportunities.

Carla Harris—vice chairman, managing director, and senior client adviser at Morgan Stanley—concludes that a sponsor "is the critical relationship of your career. A mentor, frankly, is nice to have, but you can survive a long time without a mentor. But you are not going to ascend in any organization without a sponsor."[6]

In some ways, it's hard to think through the habits that seal these relationships, because you are not the only person involved. You don't have as much control in forming relationships with mentors and sponsors as you do in building relationships with peers. However, these are some habits worth considering:

- *Mentoring from afar.* The beauty of the modern world is that we can gain wisdom from multiple resources: books, podcasts, online courses. Although it's not the same as in person, it's not a waste of time either. In addition, conferences and coaching experiences are all opportunities to receive more insight and input.

- *Join networks and groups* (digital or in person) that give you access and proximity to leaders in your field who are more experienced. And show up ready with your questions.
- If your desire for mentoring revolves around personal and spiritual growth, *inquire at your church* about mentoring opportunities.
- *Is there a chance for you to help?* Serve? Intern with leaders further along than you? Serve their projects or tasks? Elevate what they do? We sometimes perceive mentoring as little more than a conversation to help us become what we want to be. That's only part of the picture. Mentoring also includes working in the trenches of leadership and projects together and staying curious along the way and learning on the job. In this context, mentoring is more than an information download; it takes on the tone of an apprenticeship.
- *Don't wait to be rescued—ask questions.* Whether I was working with my bosses or at events, I would have questions for people. Sometimes it would be one question; for people who I was more familiar with, I'd have a list. I might not get a mentor out if it, so I'd go for a mentoring moment—a conversation where mentoring took place. But I had to be prepared for it.

- *Pray.* I don't use this as a cop-out or a platitude, but when it seems there are no mentors available or your heartfelt requests for mentoring or sponsorship receive a lot of nos, it can be demoralizing. Pray for opportunities for mentoring conversations, for sponsors.
- *Ask.* You can pretty much guarantee you will not get a mentor or sponsor without asking for one. Use your voice. Don't assume you will be discovered or that people will intuitively know your every dream and goal or your desire for investment and opportunity. It is vulnerable to ask, but it's essential.

TEAM: TOGETHER EVERYONE ACHIEVES MORE

It's understandable that as you aspire to fly in leadership, you'll want to prove yourself and your competency, especially if you're seeking a mentor or sponsor. However, doing all the work yourself is not the most effective way to fly. You don't soar solo; you fly in formation with others, such as with your team.

Your team propels you and launches you, but only if you let them. Everyone gets to play; everyone uses their talent for a cause bigger than themselves when you utilize the team around you. Sometimes we hold too tightly because we feel guilty for asking things of our teams, especially if they're volunteers. But they chose to sign up. So work with them, build relationships with them, let them help you fulfill the project you are working on, give them opportunity. Give them a safe place to try, fail, and try again.

Who makes up the team that's trying to help you get things done?

What is working? What needs improvement?

What team-building habits can you cultivate to strengthen relationships and effectiveness?

You are worth investing in. Your voice, influence, and impact are worth investing in, because every investment you make is preparation for your leadership journey.

> YOU ARE WORTH *investing* IN. YOUR VOICE,
> INFLUENCE, AND IMPACT ARE WORTH
> INVESTING IN, BECAUSE EVERY *investment*
> YOU MAKE IS PREPARATION FOR YOUR
> LEADERSHIP JOURNEY.

Everything we've worked on together in this book so far was to ground you, heal you, strengthen you for the call ahead. All the work you do on the inside—the surrender, the healing, the grit growing, and the voice lessons—are not only about you. They are about a mission bigger than yourself. You always had a twofold purpose: having a relationship with God and then representing Him in the world around you—to play your part in the Great Commission.

Which means that at some point, often before you think you are ready, all that's growing and maturing inside you—the voice and gifts that have been refined—has to step outside and take shape in the world.

Your world is waiting. It's time.

REVIEW AND REFLECT

Consider the different "wings" relationships. Note how each of the relationships make you feel, and think about the experiences that might explain why you feel this way.

Which are your strongest relationships?

Which are your weakest relationships?

What is your biggest barrier to building strategic relationships?

What might growth look like?

What is your next step to work on these relationships?

Ready to Shape a New Skyline?

(On Your Mark . . .)

Many women live like it's a dress rehearsal.
Ladies, the curtain is up and you're on.

—MIKKI TAYLOR

A GOODBYE CONVERSATION, IN THEORY

"Wait—this is the last one? We've finished already? But we've only just started getting going!"

"Well, technically, Rachel, it's been about five or six months. But yes, time's flown."

"But what am I going to do next week with the time on my hands?"

"If I remember correctly," said Bree, "time was something your life and your body could never find. Maybe you can do something with that gym membership you've been paying for all this time and show up to a class?"

The group started laughing, Rachel included. "Well, you're all welcome to join me anytime!" she replied.

"Rachel raised a good point," I began. "We've known this day was coming. We've spent a few months digging deep into our callings, finding our voices, and strengthening our leadership. But inevitably, it means we've gone to some pretty raw and vulnerable places together and in one-on-one conversations. Each of you have thought of giving up on the group or on leadership in general at least once in the last six months, six weeks, six days!" Cue laughter from all around the table.

"You're resilient women. You've each had to grapple with how hard it actually is to live into who you are. You've each had to spend some time at the cross, surrendering and letting go. So I would love to hear from each of you something you've taken away from our group that you are working on and how you're going to continue to work on it. And any thoughts you have about how our time has influenced your leadership."

"I think I'll need to say yes to who I am every day," said Bree. "I've been described with lies and labels for even wanting to lead, and I've had to put them at the foot of the cross every day instead of reacting to them or agreeing with them. Sometimes multiple times in a day! I think I have a new approach. I'm going to work on agreeing with God about who He says I am and what He says I bring. I might need to vocalize it or write it down. I've tried it a bit already, and there are good days and bad. But I need to keep affirming that God wired me with gifts for His service and stop hiding them or getting all apologetic about them."

"That's fantastic, Bree," I responded.

"I'll be using that idea too," said Rachel. "That will be good for my mind-set."

"Mine too," said Amber, taking notes on what she'd heard. Bree smiled. I noticed how much her confidence and comfort level around these women had grown over the months. I loved the way the women were now equipping one another through their stories.

I continued, "I love the idea of writing things down and taking time to speak aloud that God has given you gifts. Both parts of your approach are practical, intentional, habit forming, and simple. Who wants to go next?"

"I think I've realized that my voice really *isn't* welcome in some spaces," began Amber. "My service is welcome, my body in the room is welcome, my working extra-long hours is always welcome. But my voice, vision, and insight aren't always welcome. I know that now. I've been angry and upset about that for a long time. I realize I'm simply going to have to accept that's the truth. I also have to accept that this reality has implications. It means some big changes are ahead for me. I can't do it straightaway because of financial commitments, but I think I might be looking for a new job soon." Amber shrugged her shoulders and gave a weak smile.

Kate reached over and squeezed her hand. "We're right here with you, sister."

The rest of the women nodded, echoing their agreement.

"Good for you, Amber," said CeCe. "I'm not sure where I'll end up, but I'm going to use my voice more. My actual voice, not the palatable one I've used to be acceptable to audiences and, let's be honest, donors. It might not always end well, but I'll sleep better at night. My body's been talking to me about that for months now! I need to bring my full self to my leadership, and that includes my heritage, my story, my cultural lens, my experiences. I need to validate them, like I do for everyone else. I guess I'm saying yes to who I am in my own way too, Bree."

Bree said, "And we'll say yes to who you are, *whatever* they say, CeCe."

"I hope it's not offensive," Angela warned, "but I think the most powerful thing for me wasn't the content; it's that we met and kept meeting. I have been isolated for a long time." Angela paused and looked directly at me. I waited, wondering what else she wanted to give voice to. I could see her wrestling with it.

"No." Angela corrected herself while trying to summon courage. "Let me name it. I've been *lonely.* I've been lonely for a long time. It hurts and I've felt sad, and some days very low. I coped, I got on with my career, and I made my way through. But that didn't change the situation. And you know my story now. There weren't many women in my field, and it's been hard to connect with women at church. I just haven't been around at the times they meet—you know how it is.

"All that to say, I'm so glad I made time for this—time to be with other women who are leading. We're so different, and still I'm able to be me, all of me—a woman, a Christian, a leader. I needed you more than I'd dared to hope. I'm grateful for each of you! I'm going to encourage more women I know to do something like this or even just meet one another. We can't underestimate how important this is."

"I couldn't agree with you more, Ange," Rachel interjected.

"There wasn't always space at the table for women like me—well, like any of us, frankly. But we've had a table here for months, and it's done more for me personally and inspired me more professionally than so many of the tables I've tried to squeeze in on! We've built our own table. So for me, going on from here—I want to keep building tables. Big ones, round ones, long ones! Ones with room for women like us and not like us. These tables are places of connection but also empowerment."

"Yes!" said Kate. "Being together has rekindled two things for me: my determination and my ambition. It's like you've cleared some debris, some baggage, out of the way and now there's room to see. Did anyone else feel as though their glasses just got cleaned or something? Like you can see more clearly?"

"Oh, sis, I've got ideas like you wouldn't believe!" said CeCe, laughing. "They won't be easy. Maybe that's why determination and ambition run together—they need to! But yes, these ideas were always for a cause bigger than us. I've been reminded that even though we've done this work and looked inside ourselves, the whole point was that we'd look outside and do something about it. I feel more ready than ever to make my impact."

"Right!" agreed Kate. "It was never just about us—it was always about the cause. That's why I became a leader; that's why I got ordained. I wanted to be part of what God was doing in the world, to use up all I had—my gifts, my voice, and my time—for His call in this world. Wherever He is making all things new in the world, I want to join Him there."

The conversation continued late into the night as the women continued to talk, dream, plan, and laugh. I sat back and watched as ideas were exchanged, strategies decided, wider connections made, and contact info emailed and texted. They plotted and planned like one team. Occasionally the conversation quieted as a woman shared her fears and concerns, admitting that her courage was sometimes streaked with anxiety. They shared about how they still felt conflicted about certain areas of their lives. There were no easy answers or strategic one-liners for those issues, but there was space to listen, pay attention, squeeze a hand, pass the Kleenex, or hold someone.

I knew that when the morning came, they'd each stand facing their great unknowns. Their worlds looked different now— they were different leaders. They'd pick up the tools they'd learned to use, and they'd get to work. Their next steps would involve tough conversations, bold moves, quiet game-changing actions. Devotional habits. Risk and sacrifice. I knew that for some of them, life would get harder before it got better as they confronted challenging situations in their lives. But even then, I was still encouraged, because I knew none of them would be doing it alone. Not now, and not ever again. The group had officially ended, but they had their tools and a community helping them each carve out their unique path. My job was done.

Whether you feel it or not, you're ready for the next stage of your journey. Perfectionism be gone! But what happens next? What do we *do* next?

> DESTINY IS NOT FOR COMFORT SEEKERS.
> DESTINY IS FOR THE *daring* AND
> DETERMINED WHO ARE WILLING TO ENDURE
> SOME *discomfort*, DELAY GRATIFICATION,
> AND GO WHERE DESTINY LEADS.
>
> —T. D. Jakes

This is probably the part where we'd love a blueprint of what it looks like to step up into our leadership from this point on— a 125-point plan with a time frame! And even though we all know life doesn't work that way, it would be nice or maybe even feel right somehow, like a more valid, confident expression of leadership. As Jessica Honegger, entrepreneur and founder of Noonday Collection, wrote, "The path to success is straight, and the experience of walking it is marked by both confidence and clarity—No One, ever."[1]

This is your path, your influence, your leadership journey, so there is no prescriptive blueprint. But there are some signposts to guide you and remind you of key principles as you keep moving forward.

GET DEVOTIONAL ABOUT YOUR DESTINY

Whatever you are made for, gifted for, began in God's definition and design for you. He created you and gifted you with purpose. When

Jesus sent His disciples out into the world, He reminded them that He was always with them (see Matthew 28:18–20). So now is the time to dream—but dream devotionally. When I say "dream devotionally," I mean talk to God about the change you want to see in the world. Pray about your gifts and skills and how they might be deployed for the greater good in your community and city. If your purpose is going to be fueled by your faith, make a habit of talking to God, reading the Bible, connecting with other believers, worshipping Him. Get devotional about your destiny.

> WHATEVER YOU ARE MADE FOR,
> GIFTED FOR, BEGAN IN GOD'S
> *definition* AND DESIGN FOR YOU.
> HE CREATED YOU AND *gifted*
> YOU WITH PURPOSE.

As you dream and get a sense of where God is leading you in this chapter of your life, write it down. Keep referring to it, reflecting on it, checking in on the guidance you've received throughout the year. Keep praying into it.

But don't stop when you've got the vision. He is always with you. Hold on tightly to your relationship with God. He's there for the grit-growing days and the easy days. Hold tightly to a life where your leadership is defined by following Him, knowing it means self-denial, carrying your cross, and also having a Savior who will not hesitate to stoop down to tend to the wounds you pick up on your journey.

How will you get devotional about your purpose and calling?

ATTEND TO THE INTERNAL

The journey of owning our voices forces us to face times when we've experienced the opposite and the limits placed on us. Sometimes reflection and processing are enough to help us move forward. But sometimes the internal obstacles to our growth are entrenched and we cannot get past the past or we encounter situations that wound us again. In those situations, we need to consider the processes that will help us move forward, such as looking for support through therapy and qualified counselors.

Pay attention to see if the wounds of the stress of your life have given rise to habits and patterns you know are destructive. If you're drinking too much or your eating has become disordered and chaotic or you're medicating your stresses through prescriptions or maxed-out credit cards, join a recovery group in your area.

Make a habit of tending to the internal issues that come with life and relationships. We know leaders aren't exempt, so let's not act like they are. While you're thinking internally, pay attention to what is happening physically: your eating, your sleeping, your physical well-being. Ask yourself what your body would like to say to you, and act on it. I know I am repeating myself here. It's simply because I don't think leaders can ask their bodies that question too often!

How will you tend to the internal?

BE PRACTICAL

Alongside the devotional dreaming and internal work, our assessment of our next steps needs to be practical, because engaging practically is

devotional and internal work too! The reality of our practical lives provides a helpful filter for discerning our next steps. For example, if you
have a dream of building a business but your life is buckling under the
weight of debt and you can barely put food on the table, dealing with
your cash flow and debt is a crucial next step for your journey. If you
feel called to the medical world but have no qualifications, you need to
look at an appropriate course of study. Your next steps need to engage
with your practical realties. As you look at where you go from here,
consider your life stage and the opportunities and limitations it presents. Look at the realities of your relationships, of your mental load.
Think through your financial life and choices. Look at your goals—do
they require investment of study, time, training, connections?

What are your practical next steps?

STAY RELATIONAL

We know loneliness and isolation will debilitate our leadership, so . . .

Build that village! Work on the relationships that root and ground
you. Build consistent rhythms, not sporadic connections. Actively dismantle the work of the Great Woman Theory in your life by asking for
and receiving help.

Work on the relationships that give you wings. Join networks, build
a brain trust of peers, set realistic goals for finding the people you will
reach out to and build connections with. Decide how you will operate
when you come across environments where scarcity is the lived experience of the women there.

Accept that sometimes you will get a no when you reach for a
mentor or sponsor, but keep building those connections. Consider

being a mentor or sponsor to someone else. If you have a team, make the most of being part of one. If you don't have a team, consider if it's valuable and possible to build one around you.

Where do you need to build your village?

GET INTENTIONAL

Dreaming is one thing, and it's valuable; living your dream is another thing entirely. So consider what it would take to see your ideas and intentions become realistic steps. I love imagining and processing with other people, sharing my passions and ideas so fully that I can feel as though I've actually done something when I haven't. I've just talked about it. They are not the same thing.

What helps me get intentional:

- writing down what I am working toward as specifically as possible
- a friend who will hold me accountable, ask uncomfortable questions about my ideas and what I've done about them, and give me feedback
- a deadline that would be awkward or embarrassing to violate

What are your next steps for staying intentional?

AND KEEP REMEMBERING WHY YOU ARE LEADING

God's people have always been sent to represent Him, His values, and His good news in the world around them. It was true in the garden, and it was true of God's covenant people in the Old Testament. It was seen in Jesus's words to His disciples in the Great Commission, and it was true of the life and times of the earliest church. Wherever God's people were placed, they represented Him—whether in the corridors of power like Joseph, Daniel, and Huldah, as a farmer like Amos, a businesswoman like Lydia, a family unit like Eunice and Lois, a doctor like Luke, or a church leader like Phoebe. We are owning our voices to rise into our influence to change our world by joining in with what God is doing as He makes all things new.

Our leadership is not the end result; a better world, filled with God's love and light, shaped by His mercy and justice and grace, is. All things made new.

—————

We stand at this moment in time, in history, commissioned like the generations before us to make a difference in our world, representing the One who came to earth to make all things new. We remember women of our spiritual heritage like Deborah and Miriam, Esther and Huldah, Lydia and Mary, Phoebe and Priscilla—women who, though their paths to influence weren't straightforward or clear, uncovered ways to own their voices and step into their influence. We're still telling their stories and the stories of many other women throughout history who have uncovered their paths to influence through loss and transition, through seismic cultural shifts in their world.

I'd be lying if I said I never feel afraid and vulnerable, wondering if I'm up to the task of leadership. There are still days I'm overwhelmed, days when impostor syndrome gets a little loud in my ears.

I don't have a perfect strategy for my ideas . . . or the best resources. I cannot guarantee that everything will be successful, and that gets to me sometimes.

But I do have a calling and a faithful God whose love and power give me the courage to rise.

Now in response to His commission, it's time to own our God-given voices and rise into our influence with our tools in hand:

Unwrapped gifts
Our own voices (even if they shake) that declare our visions
Feet washed and healed by a Savior
Bodies that have been listened to and nurtured
Ever-growing grit
Strong, vibrant villages that give us both roots and wings

These tools will help us clear the debris and boulders that have inhibited us in our calls. They'll help position us and ready us to lead wherever God leads us. So like the women who went before us, let's look at our world, in all its beauty and its frailty, its desperate need and its pain, and show up with love and *do something*. Let's step up.

Let's go to our communities and cities. Let's show up in our families. Let's show up in the arts and in entrepreneurship and the corporate world and the media and the church. Let's show up anywhere we can serve and bring the renewal and human flourishing as we follow a God who is making all things new. Let's keep showing up, even when it's hard and costly and the path is uncertain. The time is now.

Let's carve out paths that are wide enough for others to join us on the journey and build tables that create lots of room for others to show up too. Let's show up boldly so that our younger sisters and daughters—with their big-picture-dreaming, broken-world-fixing, prophetic-voices-speaking passions—will find living examples to model their lives on. That they *will* see what they can be because our lives tell the stories of women who owned their voices, rose into their influence, and had a major effect on their world. And then let's take it further and show up as mentors and sponsors to launch them beyond our wildest, world-changing, culture-shaping dreams.

And let's start today.

You're ready to rise. Let's go!

I AM
READY TO RISE

My next step for *owning my voice* is:

My plan to *gather my community* is:

I'll *step into my influence* by:

Go to josaxton.com/readytorise for more resources.

Acknowledgments

This book would not exist without the kindness and sacrifice and generosity of my people. Talk about a village . . .

To my loves: Chris, thanks for the encouragement, support, and cups of tea. Tia and Zoe, you are my joy! I love watching you rise into the young women God created you to be. Keep rising, you beauties!

To all my friends—too numerous to mention (read: I'm afraid I'll miss a name!)—who have cheered me on. Thanks for every talk, text, GIF, Vox, and message on WhatsApp or Marco Polo. Thanks for your wisdom, laughter, and permission to rant. You are fabulous, and life is better with you in it.

To the Ezer Collective team and Alumni MN 2017, 2018, AK 2019, and the amazing women leaders in my coaching programs and initiatives. Your work matters; your voices matter. Thank you all for being so inspiring. *Keep going.*

To my team: Many thanks to my assistant, Jo Rapps. You've been such a blessing to me over the years. And great fun too. To Amy Chandy (you're a *total legend*) and the rest of #TeamChandyGroup. There aren't words for how grateful I am for all of you and how much I enjoy each of you. Thank you for all the Texan queso and for always letting me eat your fries when I've already eaten mine.

To my editor, Shannon Marchese. Thanks for seeing me, processing with me, and working with me. You are fabulous! Much love to every single member of the WaterBrook team. Thank you for your work, diligence, and wisdom; your kindness; and most of all your patience, because we all know that when it comes to deadlines, I clearly have *significant issues*.

And a special shout-out to Melissa Zaldivar for suggesting we take a photo and telling me jokes as it happened. Turns out it's a book cover!

Finally to the One who has always seen me, always known me, and always loved me. Who has redeemed my life, restored my soul, and invited me into His Great Commission. Thank You. Jesus, I love You.

Notes

Chapter 1: Women Who've Made a Difference

1. I lived with my aunt May until I was six years old, then returned to live with my mum. There's more of our story in my previous book *The Dream of You: Let Go of Broken Identities and Live the Life You Were Made For* (Colorado Springs, CO: WaterBrook, 2018).

2. The Commonwealth of Nations, more commonly known as the Commonwealth, is an international association of independent and equal sovereign states. Most of them are former British colonies, and the British monarch is the symbolic head of the Commonwealth (though this role has no actual political or executive power). For more information, see www.thecommon wealth.org.

3. Mark DeWolf, "12 Stats About Working Women," *US Department of Labor* (blog), March 1, 2017, https://blog.dol.gov/2017 /03/01/12-stats-about-working-women.

Chapter 2: The Cost of Disempowerment

1. Marian Wright Edelman, Goodreads, www.goodreads.com /quotes/536048-you-can-t-be-what-you-can-t-see.

2. *Merriam-Webster,* s.v. "disempower," www.merriam-webster .com/dictionary/disempower.

3. Kofi Annan, quoted in "Empowering Women the Most Effective Development Tool, Annan Says," *UN News,* February 28, 2005, https://news.un.org/en/story/2005/02/130132 -empowering-women-most-effective-development-tool-annan -says.

4. Emily Cadman, "Women Leaders Deliver Boost to Profitability," *Financial Times,* February 7, 2016, www.ft.com/content/a3267dfe -cc1a-11e5-be0b-b7ece4e953a0.

5. Sarah Gordon, "Female Leaders Boost the Bottom Line," *Financial Times,* September 26, 2017, www.ft.com/content /f88a7c58-96ff-11e7-8c5c-c8d8fa6961bb.

6. Gordon, "Female Leaders."

7. Claire Cain Miller, "Fewer Women Are Leading the Biggest Companies," *New York Times,* May 23, 2018, www.nytimes .com/2018/05/23/upshot/why-the-number-of-female-chief -executives-is-falling.html.

8. Miller, "Fewer Women."

Chapter 3: Talitha Koum!

1. I share the story of my journey of understanding God as Father in my book *The Dream of You: Let Go of Broken Identities and Live the Life You Were Made For* (Colorado Springs, CO: WaterBrook, 2018). Check it out!

2. My Sunday school teachers left out many of the problematic stories of things done to other cultures in the name of Christ that didn't represent the values of Christ.

3. There are many more Old Testament women of note to talk

about. My book *More Than Enchanting: Breaking Through Barriers to Influence Your World* (Downers Grove, IL: InterVarsity, 2012) gives a brief introduction to a few more. Also check out Carolyn Custis James, *Lost Women of the Bible: The Women We Thought We Knew* (Grand Rapids, MI: Zondervan, 2005); Michele Guinness, *Woman: The Full Story: A Dynamic Celebration of Freedoms* (Grand Rapids, MI: Zondervan, 2003); and Carol Meyers, Toni Craven, and Ross S. Kraemer, eds., *Women in Scripture: A Dictionary of Named and Unnamed Women in the Hebrew Bible, the Apocryphal/Deuterocanonical Books, and the New Testament* (Boston: Houghton Mifflin Harcourt, 2000).

4. David Scholer, "Women," in *Dictionary of Jesus and the Gospels: A Compendium of Contemporary Biblical Scholarship,* ed. Joel B. Green, Scot McKnight, and I. Howard Marshall (Downers Grove, IL: InterVarsity, 1992), 881.

5. Guinness, *Woman,* 119.

6. Guinness, *Woman,* 118.

7. Guinness, *Woman,* 116.

8. Scholer, "Women," 882.

9. These are just a few of the women leaders in the New Testament. Again, use the aforementioned list of books to find out the Who's Who of influential women in the Bible.

10. Rodney Stark, *The Rise of Christianity: A Sociologist Reconsiders History* (Princeton, NJ: Princeton University Press, 1996), 95.

11. Ava DuVernay, Goodreads, www.goodreads.com
/quotes/8661251-if-your-dream-only-includes-you-it
-s-too-small.

Chapter 5: Say Yes to Who You Are

1. Lisa Takeuchi Cullen, "The Rules According to Dee Dee
Myers," *Time,* February 29, 2008, http://content.time.com
/time/arts/article/0,8599,1718519-2,00.html.

2. Julia Gillard, "Gender Inequality in Leadership Is Solvable,"
interview by Malcolm Gladwell, July 30, 2019, in *#Solvable,*
podcast, 45:36, https://podcasts.apple.com/us/podcast/gender
-inequality-in-leadership-is-solvable/id1463448386?i=1000
445766180.

3. Lisa Sharon Harper, *The Very Good Gospel: How Everything
Wrong Can Be Made Right* (Colorado Springs, CO: Water-
Brook, 2016), 25.

4. Harper, *Very Good Gospel,* 25.

5. Michele Guinness, *Woman: The Full Story: A Dynamic
Celebration of Freedoms* (Grand Rapids, MI: Zondervan,
2003), 34.

6. For further study on *ezer,* check out my book *More Than
Enchanting: Breaking Through Barriers to Influence Your
World* (Downers Grove, IL: InterVarsity, 2012). Also check out
Carolyn Custis James, *Lost Women of the Bible: The Women
We Thought We Knew* (Grand Rapids, MI: Zondervan, 2005);
Carolyn Custis James, *When Life and Beliefs Collide: How
Knowing God Makes a Difference* (Grand Rapids, MI: Zonder-
van, 2005); and Michele Guinness, *Woman: The Full Story: A*

Dynamic Celebration of Freedoms (Grand Rapids, MI: Zondervan, 2003).

Chapter 6: A Voice Without Apology

1. Tivka Frymer-Kensky, "Deborah: Bible," Jewish Women's Archive: Encyclopedia, https://jwa.org/encyclopedia/article/deborah-bible.

2. Kathy Khang, *Raise Your Voice: Why We Stay Silent and How to Speak Up* (Downers Grove, IL: InterVarsity, 2018), 36.

3. Linda Belleville, in *Discovering Biblical Equality: Complementarity Without Hierarchy,* ed. Ronald W. Pierce, Rebecca Merrill Groothuis, and Gordon D. Fee (Downers Grove, IL: InterVarsity, 2005), 112.

4. Carol Meyers, Toni Craven, and Ross S. Kraemer, eds., *Women in Scripture: A Dictionary of Named and Unnamed Women in the Hebrew Bible, the Apocryphal/Deuterocanonical Books, and the New Testament* (Boston: Houghton Mifflin Harcourt, 2000), 67.

5. Meyers, Craven, and Kraemer, *Women in Scripture,* 67.

6. Wilda C. Gafney, *Daughters of Miriam: Women Prophets in Ancient Israel* (Minneapolis, MN: Fortress, 2008), 92.

7. Belleville, in *Discovering Biblical Equality,* 113.

8. Joy A. Schroeder, *Deborah's Daughters: Gender Politics and Biblical Interpretation* (New York: Oxford University Press, 2014), 203.

9. Schroeder, *Deborah's Daughters,* 204.

10. Janice Nunnally-Cox, *Fore-Mothers: Women of the Bible* (New York: Seabury, 1981), 50.

11. Janice Bryant Howroyd, "ActOne Group: Janice Bryant Howroyd," *How I Built This* with Guy Raz, NPR, December 3, 2018, podcast, 52:52, www.npr.org/2018/11/30/672189297 /actone-group-janice-bryant-howroyd.
12. Howroyd, "ActOne Group."

Chapter 7: Voice Lessons

1. The Brand New Heavies, "Fake," *Brother Sister,* FFRR, 1994.
2. Albert Einstein, Goodreads, www.goodreads.com/quotes /909723-be-a-voice-not-an-echo.
3. Maggie Kuhn, in "Maggie Kuhn and Women's History Month," Presbyterian Historical Society, March 11, 2014, www.history.pcusa.org/blog/maggie-kuhn-womens-history -month.
4. Brené Brown, "Listening to Shame," March 2012, TED video, 20:32, www.ted.com/talks/brene_brown_listening _to_shame.

Chapter 8: How to Grow Your Grit

1. *Merriam-Webster,* s.v. "grit," www.merriam-webster.com /dictionary/grit.
2. Angela Duckworth, *Grit: The Power of Passion and Persever-ance* (New York: Simon & Schuster, 2018), 856.
3. Duckworth, *Grit,* 269.
4. Robert Ludlum, *The Bourne Supremacy: A Novel* (New York: Bantam, 2012), 191.
5. Bethany Morgan, conversation with the author.
6. Roderick Gilkey and Clint Kilts, "Cognitive Fitness," *Harvard*

Business Review, November 2007, https://hbr.org/2007/11
/cognitive-fitness.

7. *Merriam-Webster,* s.v. "grit."

8. *Online Etymology Dictionary,* s.v. "courage," www.etymonline
.com/word/courage.

9. Gilkey and Kilts, "Cognitive Fitness."

10. Gilkey and Kilts, "Cognitive Fitness."

11. Rhitu Chatterjee, "A New Survey Finds 81 Percent of Women
Have Experienced Sexual Harassment," NPR, February 21,
2018, www.npr.org/sections/thetwo-way/2018/02/21/587
671849/a-new-survey-finds-eighty-percent-of-women-have
-experienced-sexual-harassment.

12. Chatterjee, "New Survey."

13. Simon Sinek, *Start with Why: How Great Leaders Inspire
Everyone to Take Action* (New York: Penguin, 2009), 228.

Chapter 10: The Search for Community

1. Hebrew word for *sister,* Bible Hub, s.v. "achoth," https://biblehub
.com/hebrew/269.htm.

2. Nicole Sallak Anderson, "Pretty Birds in Pretty Cages:
Could the Nuclear Family Be the Reason We're All Miser-
able?," *Medium* (blog), November 27, 2017, https://medium
.com/@NSallakAnderson/pretty-birds-in-pretty-cages-could
-the-nuclear-family-be-the-reason-were-all-miserable-46126d5
73263.

3. John Coleman, "Leadership Is Not a Solitary Task," *Harvard
Business Review,* February 5, 2014, https://hbr.org/2014/02
/leadership-is-not-a-solitary-task.

4. Thomas Carlyle, *On Heroes, Hero-Worship, and the Heroic in History: Also Essays on Goethe,* 1841, 34.

5. Bill Carmody, "The Scarcity Fallacy," *Inc.,* February 6, 2015, www.inc.com/bill-carmody/the-scarcity-fallacy.html.

6. David Meltzer, "Belief in More Than Enough: Abundance Mentality in Business," *Entrepreneur,* March 16, 2018, www .entrepreneur.com/article/310448.

7. Judith Warner, Nora Ellmann, and Diana Boesch, "The Women's Leadership Gap," Center for American Progress, November 20, 2018, www.americanprogress.org/issues/women/reports /2018/11/20/461273/womens-leadership-gap-2.

8. Harriet Tubman, quoted by Viola Davis in Luchina Fisher, "Why Viola Davis Quoted Harriet Tubman at the Emmys," ABC News, September 21, 2015, https://abcnews.go.com /Entertainment/viola-davis-quoted-harriet-tubman-emmys /story?id=33927580.

9. Ariel Scotti, "Women Are Doing Double the 'Emotional Labor' of Men—And Still Aren't Getting Enough Credit," *Daily News,* February 21, 2018, www.nydailynews.com/life-style/women -double-emotional-labor-men-article-1.3834039.

10. "New Research: 'Mental Load' Felt by Mothers Is Real and Having a Significant Impact at Home and at Work," Modern Family Index 2017, https://solutionsatwork.brighthorizons .com/~/media/BH/SAW/PDFs/GeneralAndWellbeing/MFI _2017_Report_v4.ashx.

11. "New Research."

12. "New Research."

13. "New Research."

14. "New Research."

15. "What Is the 'Motherhood Penalty'?," Modern Family Index 2018, www.brighthorizons.com/-/media/BH-New/Newsroom /Media-Kit/MFI_2018_Report_FINAL.ashx.

Chapter 11: How to Build Your Village

1. Jo Saxton, "Calling All Deborahs," Fuller De Pree Center, March 1, 2017, https://depree.org/calling-all-deborahs.

Chapter 12: The Strategic Relationships Every Village Needs

1. Sally Helgesen and Marshall Goldsmith, *How Women Rise: Break the 12 Habits Holding You Back from Your Next Raise, Promotion, or Job* (New York: Hachette, 2018), 97.

2. Sandra Bullock, quoted in Reggie Ugwu, "Sandra Bullock and Mindy Kaling Break Out of 'Actress Solitary Confinement,'" *New York Times,* May 4, 2018, www.nytimes.com/2018/05/04 /movies/sandra-bullock-mindy-kaling occans-8.html?smid=tw -nytimes&smtyp=cur.

3. Sir Isaac Newton, quoted in "Moving Words," British Broadcasting Corporation, www.bbc.co.uk/worldservice/learningenglish /movingwords/shortlist/newton.shtml.

4. Herminia Ibarra, "Women Are Over-Mentored (But Under-Sponsored)," interview by Julia Kirby, *Harvard Business Review,* https://hbr.org/2010/08/women-are-over-mentored-but-un.

5. Sylvia Ann Hewlett, "The Real Benefit of Finding a Sponsor," *Harvard Business Review,* January 26, 2011, https://hbr.org /2011/01/the-real-benefit-of-finding-a.

6. Carla Harris, "How to Find the Person Who Can Help You Get Ahead at Work," November 2018, TED video, 12:48, www.ted.com/talks/carla_harris_how_to_find_the_person _who_can_help_you_get_ahead_at_work.

Chapter 13: Ready to Shape a New Skyline?

1. Jessica Honegger, *Imperfect Courage: Live a Life of Purpose by Leaving Comfort and Going Scared* (Colorado Springs, CO: WaterBrook, 2018), book epigraph, x.

About the Author

Jo Saxton is an author, speaker, podcast host, and leadership coach. She has dedicated her career to growing leadership teams around the world and empowering women to find their purpose in their personal lives and in leadership.

Born in London to parents who emigrated from Nigeria, Jo credits her family's unrelenting work ethic and the grace of God for the bold, tenacious approach she takes to sharing her wisdom on identity, influence, and living an authentic life. She is characterized by her effervescent honesty and warm approachability, leaving audiences with practical next steps in areas that are usually a bit ambiguous.

Her book *More than Enchanting: Breaking Through Barriers to Influence Your World* discusses the role of women in church and society. Her book *The Dream of You: Let Go of Broken Identities and Live the Life You Were Made For* helps readers tackle their past, their identity, and learn how to create a legacy they want.

After founding an initiative supporting women who lead, Jo now coaches female leaders around the world through her online leadership development program, Jo Saxton Leadership Coaching, and advises organizations on how to develop and support women in leadership.

Jo lives in Minneapolis with her husband, Chris, and their two daughters.

Jo Saxton
Leadership Coaching

Thank you for purchasing my book! -Jo

Leadership takes a lot of time, intentionality, and conversation. That's why I have a created a FREE resource for you that continues this conversation.

▼

DOWNLOAD IT HERE!
JoSaxtonLeadershipCoaching.com/ReadyToRise